A CO...

CARNAGE

Glitter books

A COMPLEX OF CARNAGE
DARIO ARGENTO : BENEATH THE SURFACE
ISBN 978-1-902588-23-0
Published 2012 by Glitter Books
Edited and compiled by Jack Hunter
Copyright © Glitter Books 2012
All articles previously published by Creation Books and
reproduced by permission
All world rights reserved
CULT MOVIE FILES

foreword

A COMPLEX OF CARNAGE is a collection of essays which investigate the films of Dario Argento – ranging from **Bird With The Crystal Plumage** (1970) to **The Stendhal Syndrome** (1996) – by the application of psychoanalytical and cultural theory, thereby revealing the web of psychosexual disorders that lurks beneath the surface of Argento's *giallo* and post-*giallo* cinema.

In "Detection And Transgression", Xavier Mendik applies the work of leading cultural thinker Slavov Zizek to argue that the sexual ambiguity present in the detectives found in both Argento's and other directors' *gialli* renders them unable to "read" the signifiers which might lead them to solve each case; in "Monstrous Mother", Mendik goes on to employ Julia Kristeva's theories of female abjection and disgust to show how images of "monstrous" females in Argento's films and in related Italian horror movies can be traced back to the subversive power of the "bad" mother.

In "Totured Looks", Ray Guins utilizes feminist film theory and psychoanalysis to investigate themes of voyeurism, the fetishization of murder, and ocular destruction in Argento's films. And in "Anna With A Devil Inside", Julian Hoxter introduces Kleinian theory into his discussion of Argento, showing how Klein's theory of "object relations" can explain the crises of discrimination and identification often undergone by Argento's protagonists.

The texts are illustrated throughout by images from Argento's films, and A COMPLEX OF CARNAGE aims to provide both visual and intellectual stimulation in its trip into the latent world of one of cinema's most powerful and original film-makers.

DETECTION AND TRANSGRESSION

THE INVESTIGATIVE DRIVE OF THE GIALLO

INTRODUCTION

"I love Sherlock Holmes very much. People think he's all rationality, but his methods aren't rational at all. They're like hyper-realism in paintings... beyond rationality, almost magic"[1].

Dario Argento has openly acknowledged a debt to the classical methods of detection; in particular, the works of Agatha Christie and Sir Arthur Conan Doyle have influenced the construction of the investigative drives of his narratives. Yet these influences frequently seem at odds with the *giallo*'s obsession with displacing the actual logic and mode of detection.

What this article seeks to do is to analyze the problematic that surrounds detection in both Argento's cinema and the *giallo* in general. It will be argued that this inability to successfully detect indicates the fundamental insecurity that surrounds identity in these texts. This in turn will be analyzed using advances in both psychoanalysis and linguistics.

In terms of the *giallo*'s narrative construction, identity and detection seem to be fractured through three interdependent plot situations which this article will explore:

1. As McDonagh identifies in relation to Argento texts such as **The Bird With The Crystal Plumage** (1970) and **Profondo Rosso** (1976), the process of investigation reveals not one apparent suspect, but a second more transgressive accomplice.

2. Often related to the above is the strategy whereby the process of detection reveals a murderer who transgresses the norms of gender expectation. This device is clearly fore-grounded in Argento's cinema which is premised on the exploration of displaced female aggression. Other texts in this category include the female killer from Sergio Pastore's **Crimes Of The Black Cat** (1972). An interesting example of this strategy is also seen in Lucio Fulci's **A Woman In A Lizard's Skin** (1971). Here key suspect Carol Hammond manipulates existing gender values that equate femininity with neurosis and paranoia in order to detract a "male" police investigation away from a series of sexual murders that she has committed.

3. The process of detection as revealing or implicating the detective in the source of transgression. A key example of this is Argento's **Tenebrae** (1982), discussed below. Even when not directly revealed to be a murderer, it is marked that the *giallo* detective is often revealed as transgressive through an act of complicity. A key example here is provided in Roberto Montero's **The Slasher Is A Sex Maniac** (1972). Here Inspector Capuana allows the text's murderer to kill his own wife before arresting her after discovering her marital

infidelities.

Using Lacanian psychoanalysis, it can be argued that the *giallo*'s inability to attribute transgression to individuality embodies the "real". This is the place (marked by disorders such as psychosis) that Lacan defines as replicating an infantile collapse of identity, mastery and the self.

As such, the genre provides a radical counterpoint to the "symbolic". This is the phase which displaces the infant's ambivalent perception of its own gender and identity, providing a personality that is profoundly mediated through discourse.

Defining language as "the murderer of the thing", Lacan argued that the identity that is provided through language is essentially alienating. In particular he points to its organising and regulating of sexual difference through a series of discourses which privilege the masculine. Thus Lacan's account sees the real as a radical interspace where the oppressive hold of language falters, dislocating identity in a way which replicates the repressed infantile experience.

According to Zizek's recent work, both the phases of the symbolic and the real are evidenced in narrative forms such as detective fiction which he argues either work to confirm or deny the link between discourse and gendered identity. To posit the *giallo* as evidence of the real is to acknowledge why texts such as **Tenebrae** are so frequently seen as overriding what Franco Moretti defines as the "good rules" of detective fiction[2]. This is because Argento's film fails by containing not just one killer but two or more, which produces:

...the nightmare of detective fiction...the featureless, de-individualised crime that anyone could have committed because at this point everyone is the same.[3]

In many respects Moretti's comments prove pertinent, because the displacement of any stable notion identity and of subjectivity is fundamental to the *giallo*'s operation. Although **Tenebrae**'s Peter Neal is victimised by the Rome killer, he uses the principles of detective narration to discover his identity as that of Christiano Berti, a conservative television critic.

However, Neal's motives have little connection with legitimacy or the reintegration of law and logic. His proximity to the murders has awakened his own psychosis, and after killing Berti, Neal assumes his identity in order to continue his murderous quest.

Although Sherlock Holmes, defined by Moretti as incarnate of "a scientific ideal" is foregrounded as an influence on the detectives in the narrative, what the film reveals beneath this appeal to the principles of logic and rationality is a world governed by chaos, psychosis and gender ambivalence.

"READING" THE REAL

If **Tenebrae** is concerned with the problematic definition of identity, then this world can be evidenced by the repetition of a particular flashback sequence in which a seductive woman strips and is then assaulted in a beach location.

The scenario conflates images of sexuality and gendered violence that forms the core of Argento's imagery. Here the woman strips before a group of partially clad youths

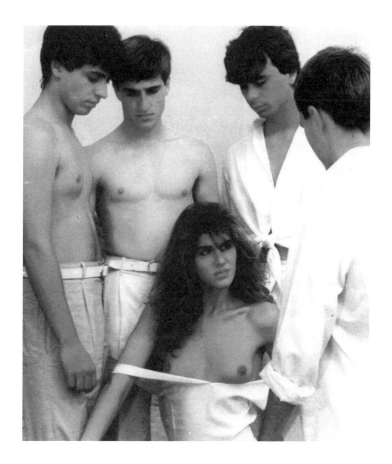

before the erotic encounter is fragmented by the arrival of another (unidentified) male. When this male is refused entry to this coupling he assaults the girl before being chased and assaulted by her assembled male lovers. The sequence ends with her forcing the spike of her heeled shoe into his mouth.

For critics of the film, this sequence seemed to confirm the text's sadistic conflation of sexuality and violence directed against the "feminine"[4]. The flashback is attributed to the killer's subjective vision[5] through two further elaborations of the sequence.

Firstly, the killer, represented by point of view camera concealed in some bushes, watches the woman courted by an officer, and after he leaves stabs her to death. When after the death of Christiano Berti the flashback is repeated, this scene of violence is elaborated, as it is revealed that the killer then steals the girl's red shoes.

Rather than being seen as exemplifying the symbolic's regulation and punishment of the woman as a sign of difference, it can be argued that the scene embodies key characteristics of the real, a psychosis which works in Argento's film[6] to wreck the link between social logic and sexual location.

In terms of the subject's relationship to reality Lacan argues that a "rent" appears in the signifying structures that have kept the subject's identity in place. This gap often reveals repressed childhood traumas such as the primal scene with the infant witnessing or imagining the act of parental coitus, and the ramifications for his discovery of the logic of sexual difference.

Importantly, as with the case study of the "Wolf Man", the scene of sexuality, and the trauma that it induces often becomes recodified as a site of sexual violence, with the mother being forced to submit to the father's sexual will. This "screen memory" often involves a conflation or recodification of the actual sites of genital difference. In the case of the Wolf Man's recollection, the childhood memory that had haunted him was recast as that of anal coitus with its implications of violent intent.

If, as the case study indicates, this basis of the Oedipal trauma is not repressed, it continually afflicts the subject through a series of scenes (such as dreams, hallucinations), which constantly disturb the individual's identity. In the case of the Wolf Man, his inability to accept paternal law was codified through a "perceptual recurrence"[7].

For instance, his dreams reordered the sexual act as one of violence, through a scenario where he believed a pack of wolves were about to savage him. As Benvinuto and Kennedy have indicated, evidence of the real also occurred for the patient through consistent fantasies and hallucinations which conflated images of castration and loss of established body image.[8]

As they note in *The Works Of Jacques Lacan – An Introduction*, one fantasy occurring when the child was carving the bark of a tree with his penknife, and was momentarily traumatised by the fear that he had partially severed a finger with the implement. Importantly, the real is not only evidenced by the imagery of castration, but by the "*unspeakable*" terror"[9] that accompanies the event. As Benvinuto and Kennedy indicate, the emergence of the real shatters the subject's use of the strategies of language classification and distinction:

The altered structure of the psychotic subject coincides with his using of language in various ways: the symbolic moorings of speech may be dislocated and he may speak in a roundabout, fragmented or confused way, or else in an excessively stylized way in which he is "spoken" rather than speaking.[10]

The emergence of the real, the fragmentation of identity, gendered body image and discourse that it produces are key in comprehending **Tenebrae**'s fragmented mode of detective narration and its preoccupation with sexual ambivalence.

The opening sequence of the film depicts the unidentified killer hurling a copy of Neal's book into an open fire, while the first murder in the film involves a shoplifter who is choked with pages from **Tenebrae**. Both actions indicate that this is a film in which language, words, grammar, syntax and logic are cut up, burned, destroyed. What these acts reveal is a fundamental instability in its core aim to attribute transgression to secure sexual identity.

As McDonagh indicates, the applicability of definition and clarity of sexual identity are replaced in **Tenebrae**'s ambivalent terrain by Neal's reviling in the realms of the "flesh". While not explicating the use of the term in a Lacanian sense, the references to the primal scene as a denial of discourse and established body image are implicit through the casting of the transsexual actor Eva Robbins/Roberto Coatti as the seductive girl in the flashback.[11]

According to Francette Pacteau, androgynous cultural representations draw on the fascinations that both artists and audiences have for that which places existing and totalising categories under stress. As a result, she concludes that the androgyne is seen as a threat to symbolic structures and its stress on differentiation of gender through language.

She notes the construction of the hermaphrodite as a figure that carries with it the symbolic signs of castration, (marked by the frequent equation of acts of violence or forced bodily transformation that accompanies such scenarios), as well as the desire to transcend gendered distinctions. This factor seems marked not only in the construction of physical pain that marks Neal's recollection, but also the sexual construction of violence that marks many examples of the *giallo*.

For instance, Monica Ranieri's psychotic reconstruction of herself beyond the limits of female lack in **The Bird With The Crystal Plumage** is accompanied by the sexual nature of the attacks on her victims, who suffer penetration with a knife. This element of female sadism is a recurrent trait in both the *giallo* and Italian horror cinema in general and can also be seen Pastore's **Crimes Of The Black Cat**. Here blind detective Peter Oliver discovers the killer of a group of fashion models is boutique owner Françoise Balli, not her male lover as suspected.

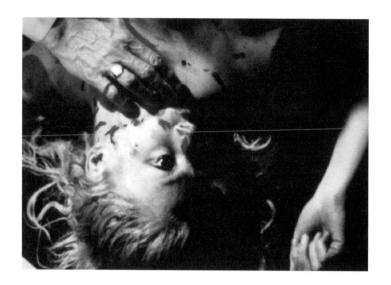

Importantly in relation to Pacteau's thesis, the motivation for Françoise's actions is premised on her "damaged" female body which she exposes to Oliver before falling to her death. She reveals that her breasts were destroyed through a car crash, thus allowing her to feel distanced from her attacks on "feminine" figures desiring her lover Victor.

In the case of **Tenebrae**, the use of Coatti (an actor whose other screen appearances stressed even more fully than Argento's film his possession of both phallus and breasts) can also be tied to the idea of gender ambivalence that Pacteau explores. The virtual suppression of hermaphroditic imagery which features the vagina as a site of difference not only encapsulates the symbolic's equation of genital difference with "lack". It also points to the ambivalent conflation of both phallus and breasts that the infant identifies as a site of physiological power. As Pacteau notes, it relates not only to the infant's equation of the phallic mother as a powerful and often threatening figure, but also to the oral gratification experienced via breast feeding:

In this light the hermaphrodite becomes a figure of excessive powers, endowed with both female and male signifiers of fertility – breast and power.[12]

Indeed, the ability of the androgynous figure to disrupt the power of difference is marked by the basis of the dream which fragments the security of Neal's identity. Just before she is assaulted, the "girl" sinks to her knees and gestures with a downward thumb movement that the (unidentified) killer does not belong in this sexual coupling.

Although critics of the film took the beach scene as further evidence of the overt (and regressive) sexualisation of women, it has another meaning within the ambivalence of identity relating to the primal scene. Rather than being degraded, her gesture can be read as a possible sign that Neal also descend to his knees and accept the reciprocity that exists between them.

Indeed, in the sequence of his humiliation that follows this shot, the denial of difference is further evidenced by Coatti's forcing of the heel of his shoe into Neal's mouth. The act (which prefigures his later fatal "penetration" by a steel monument at the end of the film) functions to link a type of circularity or series of connections between the two bodies, which are based around:

...the restoration of a less differentiated, less organised,

virtually inorganic state.[13]

To return to Argento's confessed affinity with the classical detective, theorists such as Zizek have argued that all forms of cultural representation carry with them the capacity to slide over into the troubling lack of distinction that embodies the real. It is how these elements are recuperated that decides whether they work to confirm or upturn the symbolic's drive for sexual regulation. This factor can be analyzed by discussing how the real figures in relation to the detection process of the *giallo*.

THE SURPLUS OF THE REAL IN THE GIALLO: THE DETECTIVE AS ANALYST

Returning to the study of the "Wolf Man", Zizek has noted the patient's fondness for detective fiction. This he argues informed many of the defence mechanisms that Freud had to circumvent in order to discover the root of the subject's psychosis. Freud's effective adoption of the role of detective is pertinent. As Zizek argues, the processes of deduction in works of detective fiction are analogous to those of the analyst, forced to piece together the truth from a series of fragments or clues.

As with the analyst involved in dream analysis, the fictional detective deals with acts of transgression which foreground "the impossibility of telling a story in a linear consistent way"[14]. Zizek argues that these detection processes threaten to expose the infantile trauma of the primal scene, with its focus on sexual ambivalence and loss of identity:

At the beginning, there is thus a murder – a traumatic shock, an event that cannot be integrated into symbolic reality because it appears to interrupt the "normal" causal chain... This radical opening... bears witness to an encounter with the "impossible" real, resisting symbolization.[15]

As with the psychoanalytic experience, the source of transgression in detective fiction replicates destructive infantile drives through its frequent equation of acts of sexuality and death. However if these contradictory elements are present in the classical detective tales that Argento discussed they are also clearly countered and restrained through the detective who functions to reinstate the realm of language and symbolic order.

FROM THE AGENT OF THE SYMBOLIC...

According to Zizek, this is the role of Poe's Dupin, and the "classic" detectives such as Holmes who replace him. They function to relocate and label "identity" to the evidence at scene of violent and sexual excess. For example, their success in this task is confirmed in their ability to read the "fragment" within a scene of transgression. In particular they retain the ability to isolate apparently insignificant details at the scene of crime which later proves central to the text's resolution: "Quite an interesting study that maiden," notes Holmes in *A Case Of Identity*[16], referring to Miss Mary Sutherland who has come for assistance in finding her missing fiancé. "You appeared to read a good deal upon her which was quite invisible to me," replies Watson. "Not invisible, just unnoticed, Watson. You did not know where to look, and so you missed all that was important." As Holmes continues:

I can never bring you to realise the importance of sleeves, the suggestiveness of thumb nails, or the great issues that may hang from a bootlace... Never trust general impressions, my boy, but concentrate yourself upon details.[17]

As Holmes explains, his quest to uncover the particular within the visual scene even takes on gender ramifications. For instance, he confesses that he pays particular attention to the trouser leg of a male and the sleeve of a female for "traces"[18] of gender activity during an investigation.

For detectives such as Holmes, this vital clue is usually figured in the form of a "visual fragment", that which Zizek sees as an excess, an "uncanny" surplus which upturns "the scene's totality and meaning". Importantly, what the detective has to do is re-articulate that which draws his attention, the visual, the absent, the un-symbolizable[19], and bring them back into the realm of discourse.

In *A Case Of Identity*, Holmes' reconstitution of the elements of signification is seen not only in his ability to deduce the resolution from the typeface of a letter sent to Mary by her fiancé, but also his proficiency in reading the mystery as a series of visual fragments relating to her appearance. Not only are the traces of activity Holmes seeks on Sutherland's sleeve proven to be much more than insignificant detail[20], but other deductions that he reads into her appearance such as indentations on her nose as a sign of her being short sighted also prove central to the resolution of Miss Sutherland's missing fiancé.[21]

Behind Mary's inability to see properly lies her scheming stepfather, who fearful of the loss of financial control of her earnings, did his best to shelter her from would be suitors by imposing on her a strict moral code.

When her emerging sexuality threatened this ploy, he transformed his identity into Mr Hosmer Angel, a would-be suitor for the girl. Using her poor eyesight as a means to assist his disguise, Mary recalls how they only used to meet in dimly lit night locations, where his appearance was further obscured by "tinted glasses".

By getting Mary to swear eternal loyalty to him as a precursor to their marriage, Windibank ensures that following the mysterious disappearance of Hosmer, Mary will remain unavailable to other suitors.

In *A Case Of Identity*, the indication of a coupling between a woman and someone who occupies a paternal role is clearly libidinally charged[22]. More importantly, it charts the transgression from a linguistic as well as a social position. As Holmes deduces when he reads letters that were sent to Mary by Hosmer, the wear on the typeface matches that of a communiqué that Windibank has sent to Holmes:

"It's a curious thing," remarked Holmes, "That a typewriter has really quite as much individuality as a man's handwriting. Now you remark in this note of yours, Mr Windibank, that in every case there is some little slurring over the 'e', and a slight defect in the tail of the 'r'."[23]

Although no direct punishment is attributed to Windibank, Holmes task being rather to highlight this actual transgression, the resolution seeks the reintegration of language and law. If this paternal agent possesses a speaking position, it is one which is defective, as is the typeface that reveals his hand. Indeed, Mary's comment that Hosmer seemed troubled by "infirmity of speech"[24] carries inferences of the imaginary's denial of discourse beyond Windibank's attempts to disguise his voice.

Yet it is not only Windibank who is punished, Mary does not figure in the narrative again, her fate and desire being left unresolved following Holmes' decision not to inform of her of the truth of his findings. According to Catherine Belsey, the marginalisation of the feminine via such methods forms a repeated method of resolution to the Holmes narratives.

In a universe ordered by a quest for logic, rationality and discourse, the feminine represents the threatening body, the other that must be restricted to the limits of the fictional world. As Belsey indicates, the Holmes narratives reproduce the symbolic's desire for both scientific logic and "total explicitness, total verisimilitude", through the reduction of woman as a signifier of sexual difference to a position of marginality and silence.

Indeed, it is not merely their desires that are thwarted, but often their actual ability to communicate. This is indicated in her example of *The Case Of The Dancing Men*, where the female under investigation remains either silent or unconscious for the majority of the narrative. This leads to Holmes having to crack a cypher that will not only explain the motive behind her behaviour (the desire to protect a criminal lover), but will also bring such a troublesome body back within the realm of the law.

In terms of the Lacanian construction of sexuality, Holmes remains very much the unified subject of the symbolic, who is able integrate visual[25] and verbal registers and thus provide the narrative with both coherency and mastery. Despite the difficulty of translating the iconic back into language, he "possesses the stable code, at the root of every mysterious message"[26].

If, as Zizek suggests, the format of detective fiction embodies the drives and compulsions of the primal scene, then Holmes like Dupin before him "forestalls the curse"[27] of these endless repetitions. He is able to reconstitute "the un-narrated"[28] back into discourse.

However, if the Classical Detective functions as an "armchair rationalist"[29], marked by stability both in sexual identity and access to the law, then the *giallo* provides a transgressive counterpoint to this position. It details the activities of amateur detectives, whose own identity, sexuality and subjectivity is as compromised as the murderers they seek to expose.

The classic detective such as Holmes manages to isolate himself from the source of transgression under investigation, by remaining absent from the scene of the crime when the actual transgression takes place.

However the *giallo* detective is never furnished with the same degree of security. Argento's detectives are consistently trapped by a desire to gaze in on the crime that they uncover, while the blind Peter Oliver is drawn to a whispered conversation of death and blackmail he overhears. In all cases the *giallo* detective's position is marked by a fundamental inability to distance themselves from the site of the real's excess.

To this extent the position of the *giallo* detective is comparable to a second type of investigative role that Zizek identifies. Unlike the classic, logical distanced process of deduction that defined Holmes, he defines this "hard boiled" mode of detection the "Phillip Marlowe" Way.

This references a universe where Chandler's Philip Marlowe is prevented from extricating himself from the site of sexual and violent excess because of his debt to a compromised protagonist; it is also universe where Spillaine's Mike Hammer works through a series of vendettas. Equally, recalling Todd French's reference to the "paranoid alienated seeker" of Argento's *giallo*, this is the universe where the protagonist, unable to comprehend his own gender biases, struggles in a sphere where subjectivity is itself under stress.

Unlike the classic detective, the *giallo* hero's inability to extricate himself from the site of the real is reiterated at the level of the narrative's structure. Specifically it is indicated by the failure to close off the act of crime from that of its investigation.

If, as Zizek indicates, this results in an inability to close off the tensions of the primal scene, its affects are seen not only in the psychosis which grips Peter Neal, but in the structuring of a series of sexual scenes which populate other *giallo* narratives. For instance, an example of this is seen in the construction of the amateur detective Sam Dalmas from Argento's earlier **The Bird With The Crystal Plumage**.

Although Dalmas attempts to pose in the fashion of the classical detective, he lacks the crucial ability to re-articulate this visual "symptom" within a linguistic framework. As with all Argento heroes there remains another excess, one more visual fragment beyond the reach of the comprehension of these male protagonists.

According to both Belsey and Moretti, the classical detective confirms his ability to distinguish and categorise crime by successfully integrating his investigation within the existing power structures of authority. In the case of Holmes, the narrative's drive towards mastery and control emphases the use of emerging methods of communication, transportation and forensics in the arrest of the villain. As Moretti notes:

Holmes's culture... will reach you anywhere. This culture knows, orders and defines all the significant data of individual existence as part of social existence.[30]

...TO THE DETECTIVE OF THE REAL

Although such methods of deduction are frequently employed in the *giallo*, they fail precisely because they are directed at transgressions which do not fit easily with the symbolizable.

The Bird With The Crystal Plumage employs the use of a wide range of forensic equipment from voice enhancement machines, infra red photography, microscopic analysis and identity parades all in an effort to trap the "man" Dalmas believes he has seen in the gallery.

From this constant attempt to categorise and classify, the police believe they have pinpointed accurate details of the killer's identity, such as what type of cigars he smokes, his height, taste in dress and which hand he uses to writes with. However, these processes of categorisation and distinction are proved to be futile. As Dalmas discovers, the visual fragment that forms the vital clue to investigation is based on a misrecognition that fails because it equates femininity with passivity.

As with **Tenebrae**, the film deals with the impossibility of locating transgression to identity, specifically

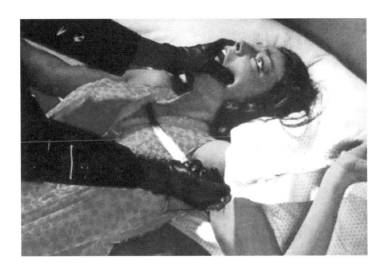

within the processes of discourse. If the processes of speech are foregrounded in Argento's first film, they function not to shore up the symbolic but draw attention to the fact that the voice as an enunciative apparatus can no longer retain the threatening surplus of the real. As the processes of voice enhancement used by Morrisini's men indicate, the text is governed by an impossibility of locating the "voice" within the specifics of identity.

This is indicated in the taped recording of a phone call from the killer to Morrisini, which forms the basis for the police investigation as to the type of man they are looking for. It is revealed to be separate from the recording of a phone call to Dalmas which forensic equipment discovers differs in its "vocal harmonic intensity".

Importantly, the voice that Morrisini and his men study (that of Monica's husband attempting to throw police off her trail) establishes the parameters of sexual difference the

detectives attempt to scrutinize, in their belief that the killer is male. Although their equipment is able to distinguish the alternation in the "grain" of the voice between the two recorded messages, it seems unable to identify Monica disguising her voice as a male in the message sent to Dalmas.

According to McDonagh, Argento's first three films are governed by a pattern of "weird science", whereby amateur sleuths attempt to solve a series of murders using scientific and criminological processes of classification and deduction.

However, their failure to integrate these findings back into any legitimate process of symbolization is confirmed by Roberto Tobias's use of optical technology in **Four Flies On Grey Velvet**. Tobias is blackmailed and stalked by an unknown assailant who claims to have evidence of Roberto killing a man in an abandoned theatre. After members of his household and family are slain, Roberto uses scientific advances in optical technology to visualise the last image on the retina of a dead victim, which he too hopes will lead to the identity of the killer.

What the resultant image reveals, an amulet with the painting of a fly imprinted on it, leads to the discovery that the killer is in fact his wife, who only married Roberto with the idea of later victimising him.

To return to Todd French's, definition of the "paranoid alienated seeker" it seems that these (characteristically male) detectives are plunged into danger in an attempt to confirm their intellectual vanities. Although presuming mastery over these situations, a sense of their social dislocation is evidenced through the ease with which they misread elements, or visual fragments of the enigma they seek to resolve.

From Dalmas' misreading of the gender of the attacker he views in the gallery, Tobias' inability to link the medical representation he captures to the fly painted amulet that his wife wears. Even Marcus Dailey's misreading of a murder scene in **Profondo Rosso**, foregrounds the fact that Argento's heroes are unable to master either the visual or the textual elements under investigation.

In forcing "his tortured protagonists, to look back and reassess what they have seen"[31], Argento draws attention to the ease with which masculine perceptions of sexuality and gendered behaviour can be unhinged. As with Dalmas, Marcus Dailey (another "artistic" foreigner living in Rome) becomes unwilling witness to the brutal murder of a psychic Helga Ullman, and similarly has to extricate himself in the

eyes of the law after being found at the scene of the crime.

As with Dalmas, Marcus remains convinced that something is lacking in his recollection of Helga's scene of death, a painting which he believes has disappeared. It is only by his returning to the scene of the crime that Dailey recalls that what he actually saw in Helga's apartment was in fact not a painting but the mirror reflection of the killer. As McDonagh notes, in both films the discovery of the truth, leads to mutilation, near death and a "displacement of the protagonist's sense of harmony with the world"[32].

Importantly, in reducing the vital clue or element that his male protagonists have to reconstruct, what Argento's narratives introduce is a duel process of criminal deduction and solution, whereby the paranoid alienated seekers' deductions are displaced by something far more threatening.

In the case of **The Bird With The Crystal Plumage**,

the scientific "evidence" pointing to Monica's husband as the killer is displaced by Monica's final assault on Dalmas when he returns to the Gallery at the end of the film. In **Profondo Rosso**, Marcus' belief that he has found evidence which incriminates his associate Carlo to the murders, is proven equally miscast when the true killer, Carlo's mother, attempts to kill Dailey following her son's death.[33]

To return to Zizek's formulation that the hard-boiled detective is unable to extricate himself from the site of transgression, it seems pertinent that this feature is often overcoded in the *giallo*. Peter Oliver of **The Crimes Of The Black Cat** is personally implicated in Françoise's violations, having lost two girlfriends to her murderous quest. Indeed, his profession as composer of the soundtracks to *gialli* which feature similar images of sexuality and death indicate an inability to establish an identity beyond these transgressive concerns.

Equally, from the very opening of **The Bird With The Crystal Plumage**, Sam Dalmas' link to the symbolic remains tenuous. If Ranieri's psychosis renders her obsessed with the image rather than discourse (she not only stalks her victims but meticulously photographs them prior to an attack), then Dalmas becomes similarly equated with the iconic.

This is implicit from the film's opening sequence, which unexpectedly fragments diegetic time and space with stop motion photography which charts the killer tracking another victim. Importantly, the subsequent murder is only referenced via an ellipsis, as the screen cuts to a black-framed diegetic insert and the victim's scream is heard on the soundtrack.

The disruption of the unity of the sound and image

band reiterates the function of the sequence to fragment the spectator's alignment to the text. Importantly, it is through this disjuncture of discourse and image that Dalmas is introduced to the text, when his associate Carlo lowers a newspaper photograph of one of the murders which reveals Dalmas in frame behind it.

Importantly, the sequence functions to establish a syntagmatic relation between the photographic preoccupations of the killer and Dalmas' problematic relation to discourse. As he reveals to Carlo in this scene, he only came to Italy to try and cure a writer's "block", but had been unable to find any work until Carlo had approached him.

Carlo hires Dalmas to produce the text for guides that accompany photographs of birds. Dalmas' link to the iconic is thus established before his encounter at the gallery. Indeed, the sequence where he and Carlo walk through the museum even prefigures it with Mussante literally coded as the "split" subject being dissected within the frame by a series of mirrored display cabinets they are walking past.

Importantly, the struggle that Dalmas views in the gallery replicates key features identified by Freud's analysis of the primal scene and its resultant compulsion repetitions. As with the "Wolf Man", the scene conflates images of sexuality and violence. This is particularly marked after the event, when Dalmas' recollections of the event constantly intervene on his love making with his girlfriend Julia.[34]

Indeed, the gallery sequence is a "scene" that not only positions Dalmas as viewer, by trapping him in the set of glass doors it also concurrently cuts him off from the processes of speech. This is indicated in his inability to communicate via discourse with either the injured Ranieri inside the gallery or

the passer-by who cannot hear the protagonist's pleas from the street outside.

Equally, its relation to the fragmentation of established body image is indicated via the reduction of the figure with which Monica struggles to a black clad figure who lacks a definable identity. This placement replicates the primal scenes recodification of the paternal agent, whom "though usually present is represented as an absence"[35].

Similarly, the gallery is populated with figures which underscore the locale as a site of both voyeurism and gendered ambivalence. For instance, during her crawl around the gallery space Ranieri positions herself beneath a statuette of an obese woman whose signs of genital difference are marked by the enormity of her breasts. Equally, the figure

foregrounds the functioning of vision through as it is constructed with distended eyes which seemed focused on Monica's body.

Other prominent iconography in the gallery includes an androgynous statuette. This embodies the fusion of masculine and feminine anatomical features of breasts and phallic shaped beak instead of the head that Pacteau confirms as subverting the symbolic's drive for classification of difference. This is the site where:

...desire is unobstructed, gender identity is that of the symbolic, the law, it is the nodal point where the symbolic and the imaginary meet and resistance occurs. The androgynous looking figure presents ...an impossibility, that of the erasure

of difference, which constructed me as subject.[36]

Although Dalmas enthuses to Julia that the mystery has managed to cure his "writing block", this reference to the articulation of discourse fails to re-establish his link to the symbolic. Arguably his proximity to the primal scene as a site of transgression functions to orientate his subsequent detection around the unsymbolizable.

Thus it seems pertinent that one of the first questions that Morrisini asks Dalmas when he finds him slumped at the scene of Monica's assault is if he is English. Dalmas' reply that he is in fact American contains resonances beyond the diegetic motivation of establishing characters information. Rather it functions to further delineate the distinction between the detective of the symbolic and that of the real.

Morrisini is linked to classical English processes of detection, indicated by his power in the realm of statistics, forensics and modes of classification and a pseudo-scientific base which keeps him structurally separate from the investigation. Contrastingly the greatest clue that Dalmas uncovers once more links him to the same "iconic" compulsion repetition as Monica.

This is the painting that artist Berto Consalti constructs as a record of Monica"s original assault, and initiates her subsequent killing spree after she sees a copy in a Rome art gallery. The picture itself redoubles the primal scene motif, depicting a sexual attack on a young girl, with her assailant's knife entering her flesh around the site of her genital area. (As with Dalmas' "scene" the assailant's identity remains ambivalent).

While Monica erects a copy of the painting in her

secret shrine where she also develops the photographs of her victims, Dalmas also constructs a photomontage of clues that he hopes will resolve the case. Argento underscores the reciprocity between the pair in one sequence by cutting from a shot of Dalmas examining a carbon copy of the painting to Monica analysing the original prior to a murder.

Importantly, the clues that lead to the revelation of Monica's true status confirm Dalmas' status within the real. For instance, his meeting with the artist Berto Consalti, who lives in filthy apartment, feasts on live cats and concentrates his paintings (such as the one of Moncia's assault) on the slicing open of the human body, indicates his location in the realm of ambivalent flesh.

If this artist's preoccupation with filth can be traced

back to the source material that Argento adopted from Frederic Brown's novel *The Screaming Mimi*, the use of this figure functions to equate the paranoid alienated hero in an infantile universe divided through both the flesh and waste matter. As McDonagh notes, although Argento extracted the character of "God" from Brown's novel, he features as Roberto's sidekick in **Four Flies On Grey Velvet**, and as a vagrant is also equated with the filth and physiology.

Thus it can be argued that the *giallo* replicates the real via this inability to locate identity to transgression, or even contain and isolate violent and sexual excess from the position of the detective. If this process of detection operates beyond the legitimacy of the symbolic (and its "classic" fictional delegates such as Holmes) then it is also marked by a recurrence of a "phallic" fatalism or masochistic acceptance of the inability to dominate the flow of the investigative drive.

In terms of the construction of Peter Oliver in **Crimes Of The Black Cat**, this is translated into a dependence on peripheral characters to either assist him or rescue him when endangered by his proximity to Françoise's actions. This masochistic intent is also seen in the recodification of Dalmas from investigator to potential victim in the closing scenes of **The Bird With The Crystal Plumage**. It is also present in the construction of male amateur detectives such as Franco Arno and Carlo Giordani from Argento's **Cat O' Nine Tails** (1971).

Here, the diegesis is once again split between the systematic examination of the modes of scientific and criminological forms of detection and their incompatibility to the *giallo*'s concentration on terrains of abjection, death and decay. The film centres on a group of scientists conducting

research into the XYY chromosome which they link to a human predisposition towards violence.

However, when the group begin to fall victim to an unidentified killer the culprit is revealed to be Casoni, one of the group who has the defective gene. As with Argento's other detectives, Giordani and Arno are unable to reconstitute the fragmented clues they uncover, as they literally represent a split between the mastery of both image and discourse that represents the classical detective. For instance, Arno is blind and dependant on his young niece Laurie for visual information, while Giordani's link to the symbolic via his status as journalist is compromised by his involvement with the daughter of a scientist involved in the murders.

Giordani even confesses the impossibility of solving the crime they are investigating commenting that it has so many leads that resembles "a cat with nine tails". However, Arno corrects his statement arguing that its resembles "a cat *of* nine tails, like the old naval whip!"

This alteration of Giordani's statement is important as it recasts the site of the investigation through a metaphor equated with punishment of the male body. Once more, this can be seen as reflecting the lack of symbolic mastery of the codes of investigation implying the crime as a site that involves the detective "ethically and often painfully. The deceitful game of which he has become a part poses a threat to his very identity as a subject"[37].

Thus it can be seen that in the *giallo*, the emphasis is not on the restriction and recuperation of the real, but its facilitation through the dislocation of identity within a diegetic space. Whereas the detective of the symbolic deals with quests such as *A Case Of Identity*, the detective of the real is prevented from even defining the parameters of such singularity.

If, as Zizek argues, detective fiction deals with elements of desire and primal sexuality which must be contained, then the foreclosure at the heart of the *giallo* threatens the annihilation of the very borders of subjectivity. These tensions are present from the pre-credit scene of **Tenebrae** where the camera pans across a page of written text of Neal's book, which links elements of suffering and humiliation with acts of "annihilation: murder".

This preoccupation with the decomposition of the human form and the identity that it encompasses, reveals the desire for death that marks the inability to contain the *jouissance* of the real. Rather than talk of the relocation of masculine identity and sexual difference, as the reviews of the film suggested, **Tenebrae** (along with other *gialli*) proclaims the destruction of the symbolic's system of self and gendered classification.

When playing the two systems of detection to the captive Giermani at the scene of Christiano Berti, Neal admits that the mystery has him stumped. As he claims: "...I've made charts. I've tried building a plot the same way you have."[38] The breakdown of the modes of structure, classification and detection that Neal admits, results from the psychosis that his latest book has unleashed. Continuing to discuss his "block" with the case, Neal concludes that the murders do not add up because someone "who is dead should be alive and someone who is alive should be *dead*".

The latter part of his statement refers not to any continued quest to destroy the female "other" as critics of the film would suggest, but to his own death, the desire for annihilation that emanates from his recollections of the primal scene. Indeed Freud's interpretation of the "fort/da" game as an example of compulsion repetition proves important in linking Neal's flashback to a notion of the death drive.

As his account of *Beyond The Pleasure Principle*[39] indicated, the child's "active" attempts to master the maternal absence via language and symbolisation often belie a fatalism which can be linked to the death drive. Freud notes the initial "passive" position of the child's feelings of helplessness and loss were often "staged as a game in itself"[40], and only later recorded as a process of mastery and control. Applying this process of visualised "recodification" to the flashback in **Tenebrae**, it is noticeable that Coatti's punishment only occurs as a *revision* of the original scene of Neal's humiliation[41].

This recodification of the primal scene, takes account of the symbolic positioning of woman as a site of "lack", but is still premised on the male subject's inability to extricate themselves from the humiliated, degraded body.

For instance, in his study of "Mr M" Michel De Musan has noted how the patient both attempted to efface the genital distinctions that differentiate sexuality, while still retaining the symbolic's definition of the woman as a site of castration. As De Musan's account indicates, the whole of "M"'s torso was covered in tattoos which defined the feminine in derogatory and sexual terms. However, by being printed on his own flesh, these statements were not distinct from his desire to incorporate those degraded physiological traits.

Thus in a series of controlled experiments "M" actually altered key areas of his external body image (such as the remoulding of his flesh into a mock vagina) to produce fusion with this female form. While still constructed as the "other", the account of "Mr M" indicates the lack of distance and mastery from the female form that embodies the real. As the patient stated "I am not a man nor a woman. But a bitch. A slut. Flesh to be fucked"[42].

It is the purpose of **Tenebrae** to position both Neal and the spectator at the site of the original flashback, the point of the writer's experience with "the pleasurable counterpart of death"[43]. If "M" experienced psychosis and sexual dislocation via the recodification of his body as an ambivalent site of flesh, then the end sequence of **Tenebrae** provides a similar pattern. Here, Neal is found wallowing in pity while Giermani verbalises the rationale for his crimes.

Linking this to the death of a girl in Rhode island during his youth, McDonagh argues that the text gives the appearance of resolving the narrative enigmas it raises. This is particularly as his statement is followed by a diegetic insert of Robbins, who appears to be addressing the audience directly.

However, regarding the text's preoccupation with the ambivalent location of identity, he notes that Giermani qualifies his statement by stating if this was Peter Neal's crime:

"If" is the key word here. For even if Peter Neal did not commit this crime, if the scenes on the beach represent something other than Neal's haunted memories of a youthful transgression... then they still dominate the fictive space setting the tone of perverse dreamy menace.[44]

As with Argento's other *gialli*, the statement followed by the diegetic insert do little to re-establish the clarity and security of the symbolic. If as McDonagh argues, these flashbacks are the "embodiment of **Tenebrae**'s driving imagination"[45], then they indicate the *giallo* to be an interspace of the real where identity and the classification of sexuality are rendered void.

NOTES

1. Argento, cited in McDonagh, p238.

2. For instance, in his review of **Tenebrae** Phillip Strick argued that the text displayed an explicit disregard for elements of investigative plotting and the processes of logical deduction.

3. Moretti, *Clues*, p239.

4. This perception of sadism in the film was a consistent feature of reviews of the film. For instance in the journal *Films And Filming* Mark Le Fanu argued: "Argento's preoccupation... seems to be with devising novel and increasingly nasty ways of killing his characters, especially when they are women. Each murder scene occasions a dazzling assemblage of cinematic effects – the camera tracks its victims who gaze back in erotic appreciation of their own vulnerability." (p36)

5. As with the vision of Casoni, the killer from **Cat O'Nine Tails**, the assailant's perspective is represented through the close-up of an iris that sub-segments the shots by opening and closing the sequence.

6. Adapted from Benvinuto and Kennedy's section on psychosis in *The Works Of Jacques Lacan – An Introduction*.

7. Freud, "Beyond The Pleasure Principle" in *On Metapsychology*, p923.

8. In her work on "Primal Scene And Sexual Perversion", Joyce McDougall has also noted "episodes of depersonalisation, bizarre body states" (p372), which accompany the traumatic re-emergence of the primal scene in patients.

9. Opcit, p153.

10. Ibid, p146.

11. The inability of Anglo-American critics to recognise this reflexive use of casting once more confirmed the negative criteria under which the film was judged. Coatti, a recognisable icon to Italian audiences, has appeared in a number of productions which have exploited his ambivalent sexuality. For example he starred with fellow transsexual

Ajita Wilson in Antonio D'Agostino's sex film **Eva Man** (1980), released in France under the title **Ambi-Sex**.

12. Pacteau, p76.

13. Ibid, p82.

14. In his *Two Ways To Avoid The Real Of Desire*, p49.

15. Zizek, p58.

16. Conan Doyle, *The Adventures Of Sherlock Holmes*, p152.

17. Ibid, p153.

18. Ibid, p153.

19. Or in the case of Mary Sutherland, re-configure not only the visual clue, but also her appropriation of discourse, which Watson defines as "a rambling and inconsequential narrative" (p149).

20. In fact Holmes argues that they indicate her genuine concern for Angel, indicating that she was working on letters to publicise his absence prior to her visit.

21. Holmes reveals in the resolution to the narrative: "You see all these isolated facts together with many minor ones, all pointed in the same direction." (p158)

22. As Holmes notes, Windibank: "...appears as Mr Hosmer Angel and keeps lovers at bay by making love himself." (p156) Commenting upon this aspect of the narrative, Moretti notes that it foregrounds the role of paternity through transgression of the Step Father. This provides a counterpoint structure to the legitimacy of lineage and a point of comparison to the actions of natural fathers. (Who as Moretti notes, along with the upstart and the noble form a recurrent criminal type in the Holmes narratives). However, he argues the tale still carries incestuous resonances: "That is the poor Stepfather is a bit like the well-known uncle enlisted by early psychoanalysis as a mask for the father." (p245).

23. Conan Doyle, *A Case Of Identity* p155. As Moretti comments on the narrative, Holmes' capacity to locate guilt via the power of

discourse clearly indicates that it is language and access to the power of communication that defines individuality. Indeed, what the resolution to the narrative confirms is that Holmes is not merely a user of such codes, but a proficient analyst able to decode mystery in terms of grammatical and syntactical structures: "I am thinking of writing another little monograph some of these days on the typewriter and its relation to crime. It is a subject to which I have given some little attention." (p155)

24. Ibid, p153.

25. Even Holmes' reference that he will "glance into the case" for Sutherland (p152) reiterates the importance of integrating vision into his investigative drive.

26. Moretti, p248.

27. Zizek, p61.

28. Ibid, p58.

29. Copjec, *Read My Desire*, p165.

30. Moretti, p246. In her book *Read My Desire*, Joan Copjec has also drawn Foucauldian interpretations to the basis of the classical detective, using Roger Hacking's research on "the avalanche of numbers" (in the form of governmental statistics) which divided citizens into numbers, classifying them along an axis such as gender, class and nationality. As Copjec notes, the period of this numerical initiation (1830 to 1848) coincides with the birth of the "classical" detective novel, and thus shares its concern with the ultimate ability to deduce with crime and murder.

31. John Martin, "What You See Is What You Don't Get", p1.

32. Opcit, p101.

33. This dual pattern of investigation and revelation is also present in Argento's **Trauma** (1993). Here the paranoid alienated seeker is represented by the film's central protagonist David Parsons, who wrongly assumes the psychiatrist of his anorexic girlfriend Aura to be

the "head hunter" killer. When the analyst is killed trying to escape from the scene of one of the murders, the real killer is revealed to be Aura's mother who proceeds to torture Parsons for his stupidity.

34. Importantly, these recollections occur via an identical pattern of stop-motion photography indicating Dalmas' inability to extricate himself from the close proximity he shares with Ranieri. The link between them seems confirmed when Dalmas begins to collect information about the killer's victims. These clues (adapted from press clippings) take the form of non-diegetic inserts of black and white still photographs of the victims' bodies, once more linking Dalmas to the violent site of representation.

35. McDougall, p379.

36. Pacteau, p63.

37. Zizek, p62–63.

38. Cited in McDonagh, p179.

39. In *On Metapsychology*.

40. Ibid, p285.

41. Importantly, this recodification involves an increasing narrativisation and control of the scenario. Arguably the original trauma of the beach scene was marked by an absence of the camera as signifying subjective vision. However, the use of point of view positioning is present in the revised scenes where Neal's presence is indicated by a point of view surveillance of Coatti from the bushes. This process of visual recodification is also central to a scene that haunts Roberto in **Four Flies On Grey Velvet**. As McDonagh notes, this takes the form of a dream (repeated four times with increasing narrativisation) that deals with a man about to be beheaded in a Middle Eastern location. As she notes, the basis of the dream begins with a long shot establishing both location and the casting of the victim's body as a site of public spectacle before the crowds. Only in later revisions does it take a more distinct form of enunciation with

increasing close-ups of the proximity of the executioner and the victim. As McDonagh notes, the final dream occurs just before Nina is revealed to be the killer. Rather than reveal his mastery over his investigation, the scenario (which prefigures Nina's own decapitation in a car at the end of the film) functions to underscore Roberto's masochism.

42. De Musan, p169.

43. Ibid, p169.

44. Ibid, p184.

45. Ibid, p184.

BIBLIOGRAPHY

Ashworth, Mark: "The Crimes Of The Black Cat", in Stephen Thrower (Ed) *Eyeball – The European Sex And Horror Review*, Issue 1, Autumn 1989.

Belsey, Catherine: 'Deconstructing The Text: Sherlock Holmes" in Bennett, Tony (Ed) *Popular Fiction, Technology, Ideology, Production, Reading*. Routledge, London 1990. Benvinuto, Bice & Kennedy, Roger: *The Works Of Jacques Lacan*. Free Association Books, London 1986.

Copjec, Joan: *Read My Desire – Lacan Against The Historicists*. October, London 1994.

De Muzan, Michel: "M", in *Semiotext(e)* 10, edition on "Polysexuality".

Doyle, Arthur Conan: *The Adventures Of Sherlock Holmes*. Wordsworth Press, Hertfordshire 1993.

French, Todd: "Dario Argento Myth And Murder" in Chas. Balun (Ed) *The Deep Red Horror Handbook*. Fantaco Enterprises Inc, Albany 1989.

Freud, Sigmund: *On Metapsychology*. London: Penguin 1991.

Hunt, Leon: "A (Sadistic) Night At The Opera – Notes On The Italian Horror Film". *The Velvet Light Trap* No.30, 1992.

Jones, Alan: "Opera" in *Cinefantastique* Vol 18, No 2–3 March 1988.

Le Fanu, Mark: "Tenebrae" in *Films And Filming*, September 1983.

Martin, John: "What You See Is What You Don't Get", in Pierre Jouis (Ed) *Fantasy Film Memory* No.4–5: Directed By Dario Argento. Gothic, Paris 1991.

McDonagh, Maitland: *Broken Mirrors Broken Minds, The Dark Dreams Of Dario Argento*. Sun Tavern Fields, London 1991.

McDougall, Joyce: "Primal Scene And Sexual Perversion" in *The International Journal Of Psychoanalysis* Vol 53 (1972).

Moretti, Franco: "Clues" in Tony Bennett (Ed) *Popular Fiction, Technology, Ideology, Production, Reading*.

Pacteau, Francette: "The Impossible Referent: Representations Of The Androgyne" in Burgin Victor, Donald James, Kaplan Cora, (Eds) *Formations Of Fantasy*. London: Routledge, 1986.

Palmer, Jerry: *Potboilers*. Routledge Press, London 1991.

Poe, Edgar Allan: *Tales Of Mystery And Imagination*. Wordsworth Editions, Hertfordshire 1995.

Strick, Philip: "Tenebrae" in *Monthly Film Bulletin*, May 1993.

Williams, Linda Ruth: *Critical Desire – Psychoanalysis And The Literary Subject*. Edward Arnold, London 1995.

Zizek, Slavoj: *Looking Awry*. October Press, Massachusetts, 1991.

TORTURED LOOKS

DARIO ARGENTO AND VISUAL DISPLEASURE

INTRODUCTION

Whether crawling along a floor or tracking up the sides of a building, Dario Argento's sinister and ever restless camera draws fervent devotees. To accompany his wandering eye, Argento also provides rich, idyllic scenes in which to view. Well known motifs include: the ever famous black leather gloves, resplendent red hues of blood, glistening knife blades, masked killers, eerie aggressive soundtracks, tortured eyes, and of course murder. His quarter century of film directing partly locates itself neatly into a horror "sub-genre" known as the *giallo*. This term, first made famous by Italian director Mario Bava, literally means "yellow" and stems from Italian crime books which were traditionally bound in yellow covers. Whereas traditional horror and mystery films emphasise a struggling yet surviving protagonist who overcomes tragedies or solves the horrific conundrum, the *giallo* places equal (if not more) importance on the actual method of killing as well as solving the crime. Argento has however, imbued the *giallo* with a distinctive aura all his own.

His characters usually suffer from a repressed libido. They grow twisted and deranged, leading to total immersion into madness. Male characters are ill-suited to traditional notions of the phallocentric hero. That is, they lack the power and the authority commonly associated with men in horror films. Female characters also defy simple categorisation. Both genders partake in killing, both become victims. And in some cases, the murderer's gender is revealed during the closing minutes of the narrative. When a crime is dissolved, a sense of unsettlement lingers because Argento denies the sense of emotional release associated with horror films. Boundaries between good and evil are so unclearly demarcated that one is left to wonder which position has really been conquered while the films' protagonists are frequently left both mentally and physically scarred. Finally, by means of recurring motifs and a dynamic gaze, Argento's *giallo* builds intricate webs of subjectivity between the characters and spectators of his films.

I choose here to discuss **Profondo Rosso** and **Opera** in relation to psychoanalysis and feminist film theory because these two fascinating texts most clearly illustrate the relationship of subjectivity to "fetishisation" and the gaze. As briefly mentioned earlier, Argento uses his camera to a dynamic end. The use of point of view shots (I-camera) have virtually become a trade mark of "slasher" films that reached their peak during the mid-'80s. The I-camera is used in order to illustrate the killer's visual perspective. Argento takes this process to extreme measures by constantly switching the point of view between characters. In some cases the viewer is unsure who is doing the looking. And once a visual perspective is established the possessor of sight is punished for looking. Punishment is dealt by torturing the spectating eye of both characters in the film and audiences watching the film. Argento leaves the characters amongst a paradox of sight, both the characters and human spectators are forced to look while at the same time castigated.

FETISHISM

Whether female or male, killers in **Profondo Rosso** and **Opera** surround themselves with fetish objects. Freud (1977) states that the fetishised object acts as a substitute for the male "penis" which the castrated woman wishes to possess. Rather than adopt Freud's notion of penis=phallus, Lacan holds that the phallus is a symbolic structure. This Weedon (1987) describes as a Lacanian reworking of Freud ultimately ending in the phallus as the "signifier of sexual difference, which guarantees the patriarchal structure of the symbolic order" (Weedon 1987:53). Stam *et al* (1992) distinguish Freud and Lacan's positions by asserting that fetishism does not pertain to a real woman without a penis, but to a "structure in which symbolic relations, already constituted as meaningful, are put into play" (Stam *et al* 1992:149). Argento stresses the phallus by visually dwelling on fetishised objects. To illustrate, in **Opera** the camera investigates the killer's "tool box" and gently tracks the blade of a huge knife from the bottom to the top thus illustrating its enormity and power. **Profondo Rosso** shares a similar scene as the camera slowly tracks over marbles, bits of thread and toy dolls before stopping at a switchblade. The camera then proceeds to erotically inspect the switchblade, exploring along its slender shaft ending at the tip of the blade. Such emphasis on phallic signifiers highlights their purpose, i.e. to penetrate.

The traditional *giallo* demands that one observe the numerous murders, thus placing strict attention on acts of violence. I consider this a film fetishisation of murder (most prominent in **Opera**) which surpasses traditional notions of object fetishism of which Argento makes free and frequent use. In some cases Argento wants the spectator to witness the knife going in and out of the body or simply view the knife in the body. Creed (1986) comments that the action of stabbing a knife into a woman is to symbolise a sexual act. For example, during the scene at Carlo's primary school Carlo stabs Gianna with a switchblade. Marc finds Gianna resting upright against a wall complete with knife in stomach. The knife is left intact, so the viewer can see that she has been penetrated. However, Argento's knife is not gender specific. It penetrates both male and female bodies at the hands of both male and female killers. In other words, both men and women battle for control of the phallus.

A variety of readings have been forwarded to account for the phallic significance of murder. To cite an instance, Creed (1986:71) states that:

Woman's body is slashed and mutilated, not only to signify her own castrated state, but also the possibility of castration for the male. In the guise of a "madman" he enacts on her body the one act he fears most for himself, transforming her entire body into a bleeding wound.

If the victim is a woman, body mutilation is to signify her existing castrated state. Whereas if the victim were a man and the killer a woman, her actions are to be read as attempts to castrate the male by possessing the phallus and using it against her victim.

Creed (1993) argues that the fear men possess from castration has forced them to identify woman as the castrating agent. Due to Lacan's emphasis on the phallus as symbolic and not actual in the form of the penis, neither women nor men can obtain the phallus. The quest for phallus possession is an attempt to create the mythical unified whole that we lack. (Sarup, 1993).

In **Profondo Rosso** the young Carlo watches his mother stab his father. After the stabbing, the symbolic knife is left at the feet of Carlo, he then clutches the knife in his own hand. In a symbolic exchange of power, Marta uses the phallus signifier to free herself from the oppressive father figure. Then, the dying father gathers enough strength to pass the phallus in the form of the knife onto his son. Unsure how to respond, Carlo stares at the knife. Freud (1977) claims that the child witnessing his parents engaging in coitus develops a sadistic view of sex in which a power relation exists where the stronger partner forcefully penetrates the weaker. Carlo's primal trauma could then be considered the murderous act which carries a more literal and lethal version of parental sexual signification.

One learns that Carlo chooses men as his preferred sexual partners. During Marc's discovery of this fact, Carlo taunts; "Now you know I'm a faggot" (U.S. version) and "Now you know that I have perverse sexual practices" (Italian version). Carlo's lifestyle causes a conflict within himself. According to Lacan, Carlo sees himself in his father as other, hence identifying with his father's castrated state. Marta destroys the symbolic reserved for the father and through murdering other people attempts to possess the phallus. Carlo now has his mother entirely to himself, but rejects her out of fear of castration choosing to remain among men.

Two additional motifs used to connote Carlo's childhood experience while recreating Marta's murderous

experience are toy baby dolls and the eerie nursery rhyme. Both act as signifiers for the killer and their murders. Before Amanda Righetti is scalded she finds a toy baby doll hanging from a noose in her house. In **Profondo Rosso**, Marta uses a mechanical doll marking the threat of death to Professor Giordani. He is further symbolically castrated by having his teeth bashed out on a marble mantle. Silverman (1983) forwards Lacan's notion that a child's play toys are used as an object to suffice their missing component. The killer's use of the dolls confuses matters, because under ordinary circumstances, the toys would be equated with Carlo, but Marta uses them to mark death. Dolls might be viewed as a form of confession by Marta for the murdering of Carlo's father. In discussing fetishism, Freud (1977) states that a fetish object is adopted due to the overwhelming horror of seeing the absence of the penis from the woman. Objects that come to be fetishised act as a substitute for one's lack. Creed (1993) goes on to state that the object in question does not necessarily have to be a "penis-symbol". The object in question is appropriated as the last object in the child's visible field before he views the woman's genitals. A baby doll was present during the murder Carlo was witness to. Marta has stolen fetish objects from Carlo and uses toys and music to recreate the original murder scene. Recreating the murder scene allows Marta to unleash the madness she represses. The music might serve as an example of Freudian displacement. Marta actually plays the song before killing. This process provides the film with a nostalgic feel because the music continually acts as mnemic traces foreshadowing the revelation of a horrible childhood.

THE GAZE, VISION AND SPECTATOR

The camera itself possesses a phallic quality. Balun (1991) reveals that the serpent-like movement of Argento's camera takes the viewer through winding tunnels, up twisting staircases, into dark damp passageways, penetrates mutilated bodies, and allows the spectator a killer/killed point of view. Forceful activity on the part of Argento's camera demands attention on the part of the spectator. Such a camera coupled with Argento's directorial intention is masculine and sadistic. The camera is powerful. It serves as authority over the spectator's experience. We are nearly as subject to Argento's wilful camera as Betty to Santini's sadism. Under this analysis, Creed (1993) would be correct in noting that horror films which promote identification foster a masochistic form of looking. Because Argento draws the viewer into his film and once in, punishes them for watching. The spectating subject as associated with the cinematic apparatus witnesses the killer's deeds while his or her field of vision is infiltrated to construct and maintain the masculine gaze.

Connecting the spectating subject's process of identification to the actual act of looking is what Metz (1975) refers to as primary cinematic identification. Viewer perception is directed by camera movements. Point of view shots allow spectators to witness (first hand) the killer's actions. Usually as Stam *et al* (1992) illustrates, the point of view shot creates an empty space thus allowing the cine-spectator to occupy as otherness. Argento exceeds this type of identification by taking spectators into the killer's psyche. By showing the pulsating brain, one visually experiences the killer's adrenalin rush. The camera itself builds upon this experience by mimicking the pulsating motion of a throbbing brain.

Betty and Carlo are victims of visual childhood trauma. However, other characters in **Profondo Rosso** and **Opera** suffer the consequences of a curious eye. Most notably, Mira (Betty's stand-in mother figure), who is shot point blank as she peers into a peephole to catch a glimpse of the killer. The spectator actually views the bullet (slow motion close-up) fired from a gun, pass through the peephole and blast through Mira's eye socket only to exit out the back of her head. The killer punishes those who attempt to capture him/her in the gaze. The killer attempts to free him or herself from surveillance by going to its source – the vulnerable eye.

The destruction of eyes in the film is not distinct to

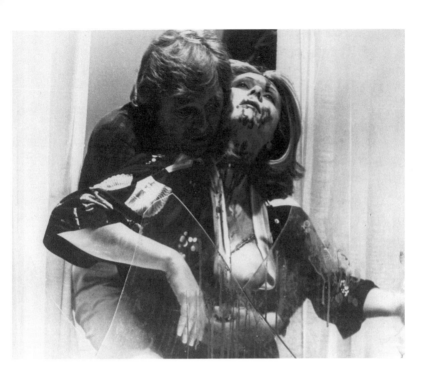

Argento. Other Italian horror directors such as Lucio Fulci use the delicate organ as a "money shot" in their films.

One of the greatest eye mutilation scenes ever to appear in film, would no doubt have to be Buñuel's **Un Chien Andalou** (1928). Williams (1994) argues that what makes the slicing of the eye appear gruesome and horrific is that the camera allows the spectator to actually watch the event in its entirety without editing right before the tragic moment. The eye itself is the ideal organ for destruction. Williams (1994) reminds us that the organ itself is grotesquely vulnerable and highly sensitive. In these respects, the eye is very similar to the penis. Both are exposed organs, very sensitive. If looking being fostered in Argento films is masculine, then hurting the eye could be equated with castration. The eye itself houses characteristics such as tears, protein deposits, and discharge that lend themselves to elements of disgust that are also common in horror films, namely associated with a monster. Presenting his theory of horror, Carroll (1990) holds that in order for a film to be considered a member of the horror genre it must possess the element of disgust. Eyes by their nature are already regarded as horrific, to actually witness the organ's destruction generates further fright and commentary on spectatorship.

It has already been established that eyes play an important role in Argento films. What remains to be explored is whether what they see generates the attention they suffer. One aspect of sight is Argento's use of his camera. McDonagh (1991:8) describes:

*Unrestrained by strictly narrative concerns, the camera reflects no point of view save its own as it creeps across the facade of a sharply angled building for a startling two and a half minutes or hovers over two girls in a baroque swimming pool (**Suspiria** 1977), their pale legs floating like seaweed beneath the water's rippling surface.*

What distinguishes Argento from other directors is that his camera continues to film where others stop. In regards to point of view, I have to disagree with McDonagh, the camera does indeed reflect various points of view – only for a limited amount of time in relation to characters. For example, the point of view is shared between killer and victim. But the point of view is also adopted by others not immediately engaged in struggle such as: ravens, other characters and unknown voyeurs. This allows the spectator access to various perspectives of cinematic identification.

Argento's own privileged position as a director, is his personal vehicle of representing his own desires. For example, he characterises his "look" by constituting Betty as an object of the desiring gaze. Betty is looked at from a voyeuristic (perverse) perspective by Santini, the camera, and the spectator. Whereas her way of seeing is more scopophilic i.e. intended to be pleasurable. My support for claiming that Argento's camera maintains the phallocentric gaze comes from Argento himself. He is known for his infamous statement, "I like women, especially beautiful ones. If they have a good face and figure, I would much prefer to watch them being murdered than an ugly girl or man". (Clover 1987:111). What stands out in Argento's statement is the word "watch". His ocular obsession with "watching" beautiful women is shown to the spectator so that we can "enjoy" and accept his sadistic, voyeuristic pleasures as our own. The act of looking is strongest in **Opera**. The film is strongly absorbed with seeing and what is seen (Martin, 1991). The character of Betty is physically attractive. Her appearance is what the killer comes to fetishise as a signifier of his lack. In two scenes Betty is abducted, bound, gagged and forced to watch Santini murder his friends. Santini himself is also a deranged pawn of vision. He also was forced to succumb to the gaze of his lover, who happened to be Betty's mother. She would seduce Santini into killing other women while she watched. Her appetite for sadism grew and becoming more and more selfish, she wouldn't allow Santini to touch her. He eventually kills Betty's mother. Santini constructs Betty's role

as Lady Macbeth (Betty's mother was also an opera singer) as his lost other that has returned for him to win back. He hopes that by forcing Betty to watch, she will come to adopt the desires of her mother.

In the area of ideology, Argento's camera is very much masculine hence maintaining the male sexual gaze that Mulvey (1975) describes in her article "Visual Pleasure In Narrative Cinema". The gaze incorporates both men and women by showing the spectating subject how women are to be looked at. The masculine gaze attempts to legitimise itself by constituting its vision as the desire of the human spectator. Thus as Kaplan (1983) explains the gaze forces the spectator to identify with men while placing women in opposition. A particular scene of **Opera**, specifically focuses on Betty as both watcher and watched. The subject of violence is unclear. Betty's eyes are forced open by notorious needles, forcing her to watch the killer's deeds. The point of view and reverse shot used in this scene supports Mulvey's claim that spectatorship is from an active male perspective that watches a passive – in this case bound, tortured and displayed – female. Betty is purely meant to be watched, the fact is enforced by Santini placing her in the display case. The spectator watches Betty and watches Betty watch Santini. Mulvey also states that the three looks – "the camera, the characters, and the spectator produce a specific, eroticised image of the woman, naturalising the 'masculine' position of the spectator and the pleasures that entails" (Stam *et al* 1992:175). Betty's point of view is distorted by the needles taped to her lower lids. This is the very perspective that Argento allows the spectator. We watch Betty as she at the moment would be watching us. Argento also uses these scenes as playful commentary on those fans who watch horror films through covered eyes. He professes to hate when people turn their heads or cover their eyes during the gory scenes of his films. Williams (1994:16) comments on this scene:

Her eyes bleed a little, the real violence comes from the fact that she cannot close them. Who is the focus of the violence is not clear, others are being killed, but Betty's violation is primary – she is made to watch, on penalty of losing her eyes themselves, which is worse then the deaths taking place before her.

This scene's creepy content ranks among the most brutal and powerful shots in the film. Although Stephen's death was malicious and bloody, it was fast-paced. Stephen was in a sense an easy victim. He offers little resistance. The slaying of

Julia takes on a new dimension. She puts up a fight and when she is eventually defeated – after subjecting the killer's face to her gaze – her death still manages to cause Santini aggravation. She swallows the bracelet. Santini has to slowly and with detail cut open her throat to retrieve it as her lifeless eyes stare aimlessly. Incidentally, Betty remains tied and tortured during the entire scene. Creed (1993) believes that scenes which appear horrific unsettle the "unified self" of the viewer. The spectator may break identification and sight by turning away or covering their eyes. Betty isn't so fortunate.

SUBJECTIVITY: CHARACTER IDENTITY – ROLE OF ILLUSION AND MIRROR STAGE

Betty's pain and agony stem from having to watch. Marc's

dilemma is having to remember the vital clue that he saw the night of Helga's murder. Marc searching for the eerie illusion of his subconscious reveals itself to be a reflection in a mirror. McDonagh (1991:118) describes the scene in Helga's apartment:

The hallway of Helga Ulman's apartment is lined with small, mostly round canvasses: they depict a veritable sea of Munchian faces, pale, ghastly, and anguished. In a niche is a mirror in a frame, and in this mirror Marc sees Marta's chalky face, surrounded by reflections of the painted faces hers so resembles.

When the police arrived at Helga's apartment, he was certain that the police had moved one of the paintings. Marc begins to investigate the crime believing the lost clue to be a painting, that somehow will reveal the missing clue. In an ironic way, Marc is partially correct. A child's drawing does reveal Carlo, who is covering up for his mother. Only when Marc returns to Helga's apartment and stands in Marta's position, does he identify with her reflection.

The mirror stage in Lacanian psychoanalysis marks the point when the child attempts to identify with its reflection in the mirror (Weedon 1992). Laplanche and Pontalis (1973) define the mirror stage: "the infant perceives in the image its counterpart or in its own mirror image – a form (Gestalt) in which it anticipates a bodily unity which it still objectively lacks" (Laplanche & Pontalis 1973:251). Observing itself in the mirror or another person (the mother's face) the child recognises objects that are different than he or she. This acknowledgment lends itself for identifying one as a self.

Thus the child comes to recognise itself from another. The process of identifying with the ideal image is the child's first attempt to supplying meaning to its lack (Grosz 1990). The use of mirrors in **Profondo Rosso** coincides with the Lacanian theory of identity.

Black (1993) argues that the use of mirrors in **Profondo Rosso** is to emphasise the criticalness of illusion. Entering Helga's apartment in an attempt to remember. Marc spies the mirror which he didn't realise was there. Marc stands in the position that Marta stood in on the night of the murder. The spectator sees Marc's reflection placed in the same painting as was Marta's ghostly reflection. Marc stares at his reflection identifying with the image, he sees himself cast as the murderer. Marc sees himself in the murderous other. After Marta attacks and is decapitated, the film ends with Marc staring into a pool of blood. The viewer is left watching Marc's reflection in the crimson pool. Carlo once occupied this position. He however, gazed into his father's blood, Marc stares into his mother's. Marta may in fact be dead, but Marc's reflection leads us to ponder if the event has turned him into a madman. Has Marc chosen his identity by assimilating the image of the other as his own? The reflective pool and Marc's narcissistic gaze may very well transform the image of otherness into a reflection of what Marc has now accepted as the self.

The mirror image draws parallels between Marta, Marc, and Carlo. Marc and Carlo have an emotional relationship. Both men suffer from an uncertain and "unbalanced" sexuality. Carlo's lifestyle causes him disgust and despair in the eyes of his other. Marc who also seems to be sexually repressed views sex and for the most part,

il GATTOa NOVE CODE

Suspiria
un film di DARIO ARGENTO

SALVATORE ARGENTO presenta

un film di DARIO ARGENTO

JESSICA HARPER   STEFANIA CASINI

Suspiria

FLAVIO BUCCI   MIGUEL BOSÈ
BARBARA MAGNOLFI   SUSANNA JAVICOLI   EVA AXEN
con ALIDA VALLI nel ruolo e con JOAN BENNETT
direttore della fotografia LUCIANO TOVOLI
musiche dei GOBLIN con la collaborazione di DARIO ARGENTO
edizioni musicali BIXIO CEMSA (Milano)
un film prodotto da CLAUDIO ARGENTO
per la SEDA Realizzato S.p.A. (Roma)
distribuzione P.A.C. PRODUZIONE ATLAS CONSORZIATE
regia di DARIO ARGENTO

TECHNOVISION   TECHNICOLOR

決して ひとりでは見ないでください

あなたたち全員をぶちのめす！！
会館立体移動装置
ザ・カム・ムーブ・サウンド
SUSPIRIA

サスペリア

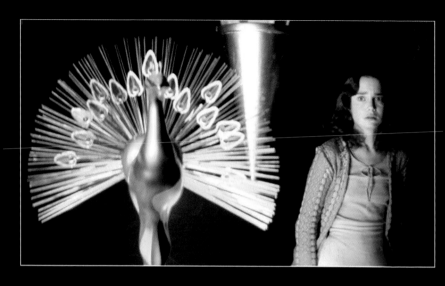

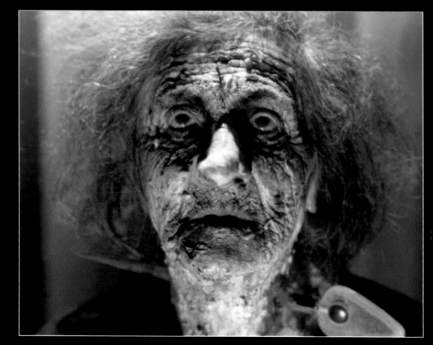

Inferno

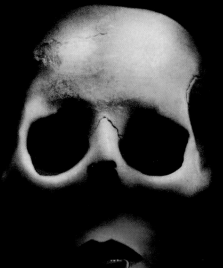

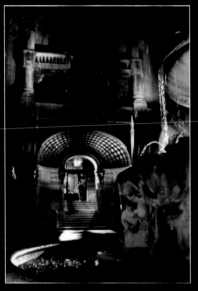

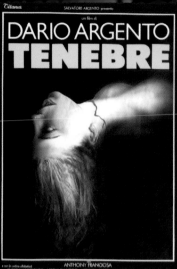

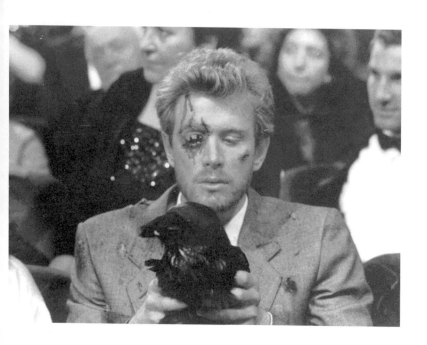

women, as dominating. McDonagh (1991) states that both Marc and Carlo are reduced to helpless impotent characters. Carlo is constantly drunk, falling down. He seeks help and direction from Marc. Marc appears to express genuine fatherly concern for Carlo and enjoys his company. The character Gianni proves to be Marc's sexual other. She is forceful, up front and a very sexual character. Marc being ineffectual is completely dominated by Gianni. She controls and intimidates him. During their second meeting, Gianni tells Marc that at the present time she doesn't have a boyfriend. Marc doesn't express interest, nevertheless, she selects him as her lover.

Argento purposely illustrates their unbalanced power relation. She beats him at arm wrestling in an answer to Marc's comment that women are physically weaker. Gianni saves Marc from the burning house. Marc is further humiliated by the fact that Gianni always drives and her passenger seat is positioned lower so that Marc can barely see over the dash board. The women in Marc's world, one a murderer and the other "sex crazed", act as constant reminders of Marc's symbolic castration. One being the castrator and the other a reminder of the women's castrated state.

Betty also suffers a similar fate. During a "needle" scene, Santini holds a mirror up to her field of vision, so that she can view her tortured state. At this stage in the film Betty is horrified and disgusted at her appearance. She resists by trying to look up. Betty is refusing to adopt the mirror image as her identity. At the end of the film, Betty freely stops and watches Santini repeatedly stab Marco. Betty could have continued to run while Santini was preoccupied with Marco, instead she elected to remain and once again watches Santini's gruesome performance. After Santini finishes, Betty acts as if this sight has awakened a secret sadistic part of her that makes her just like her mother (she plays the role in order to escape from Santini). The text never reveals Betty's self-proclaimed reasons for describing herself as "frigid" or a "disaster in bed". Before the murders begin she seems quite content in her position. After being subjected to the brutality and throughout the rest of the film, she naturally warms to Marco – a known sadist. Marco expresses his sadism by directing horror films.

Her changing attitude seems to lead the viewer to believe that Betty is more like her mother than she realises. The case is further complicated by the fact that Argento decided to release the film with two different endings. In one ending, once Santini is apprehended, in an almost too convincing and highly exaggerated performance, Betty assures the spectator that she loves life, and proceeds to free a trapped lizard. She claims the world is hers to love. The other version ends when Santini is restrained by Interpol. The dual endings, one with Betty heading towards insanity and the other allowing her to maintain her faculties allows the spectator to draw his own conclusions. Whether or not she desires the lust crimes of her mother is uncertain.

CONCLUSION

In reflection, the end result is a corpus of film texts simultaneously exploring and creating the relationship of spectatorship to film subjectivity. Argento's film technique, especially his camera, extend to the spectator perspectives frequently ignored by other directors. His sadistic gaze operates to position the spectator within the madness. Numerous uses of point of view shots and emphasis on mirror images allows the spectator not only the opportunity to witness brutality, but to actually lose and define themselves while adopting a role. Thus identifying with the scopic division of watcher and watched as well as violator and victim. These films consequently inhabit a special niche in the history of film along with such precedents as Hitchcock's **Vertigo**, which allows the spectator to experience vertigo. However, this identification privilege reserved for Hitchcock's protagonists is also extended to Argento's villains. We experience the dark and evil aspects of film subjectivity as poignantly and directly as the good, that is, when Argento bothers to differentiate the two. Spectators are juggled back and forth, uneasily "resting" at the film's conclusion.

Stunningly executed murders are now open to cinematic spectators via access to visual facilities and the anonymity of the black gloves which wield the flashing blades. The overvaluation of eyes, knives and various other objects including the female body, fetishises the way spectatorship is constructed as part of the cinematic apparatus. In effect, these films serve as a kind of twisted presentation of relationships between what we are shown and what the discourse of the film tells us we see.

BIBLIOGRAPHY

Balun, C. (1991), "Dario Argento: Face To Face", *Deep Red*, Special Edition, Number 7.

Black, A. (1993), "Deep Red", *Necronomicon*, 3, p15–21.

Carroll, N. (1990), *The Philosophy Of Horror*, Routledge, New York and London.

Clover, C. J. (1987), "Her Body, Himself: Gender In The Slasher Film", *Representations*, p20, (Fall).

Creed, B. (1986), "Horror And The Monstrous Feminine – An Imaginary Abjection", *Screen*, 27(1):44–72 (January–February); (1993), *The Monstrous Feminine*, Routledge, London and New York.

Freud, S. (1977), *On Sexuality: Three Essays On The Theory Of Sexuality And Other Works*, Penguin, Harmondsworth.

Grosz, E. (1990), *Jacques Lacan: A Feminist Introduction*, Routledge, London and New York.

Kaplan, A. (1983) *Women And Film: Both Sides Of The Camera*, Methuen, London.

Laplanche, J. and Pontalis, J–B. (1973), *The Language Of Psychoanalysis*, W.W. Norton, New York.

Martin, J. (1991), "Dario Argento: A Deep Red Opera", *Fantasy Film Memory*, Gothic, Paris.

McDonagh, M. (1991), *Broken Mirrors/Broken Minds: The Dark Dreams Of Dario Argento*, Sun Tavern Fields, London.

Metz, C. (1975), "The Imaginary Signifier", *Screen* 16(2):14–76 (Summer).

Mulvey, L. (1975), "Visual Pleasure And Narrative Cinema", *Screen* 16(3):6–18 (Autumn). Sarup, M. (1993) *An Introductory Guide To Post-Structuralism And Post-Modernism*, University of Georgia Press, Athens.

Silverman, K. (1983), *The Subject Of Semiotics*, Oxford Press, New York.

Stam, R., Burgoyne, R. and Flitterman-Lewis, S. (1992), *New Vocabularies In Film Semiotics*, Routledge, London and New York.

Weedon, C. (1987), *Feminist Practice And Post-Structuralist Theory*, Blackwell, Oxford.

Williams, L. R. (1994), "An Eye For An Eye", *Sight & Sound* 4(4):14–16 (April).

FROM THE MONSTROUS MOTHER TO THE "THIRD SEX"

FEMALE ABJECTION IN THE FILMS OF DARIO ARGENTO

"My daughters, together are a mother to me. Without them I would be lost."[1]

INTRODUCTION

Dario Argento is here commenting on the casting of his daughter Asia as the confused heroine Aura, of his 1994 film **Trauma**. The maternal reference in his statement is important as the narrative concentrates on the "headhunter" killer who decapitates the surgeons responsible for the death of her infant son. In this respect, Argento reveals his murderer Adriana, to be a "monstrous" mother whose vengeful actions provoke fear and disgust in the assembled protagonists. The finale depicts the killer presiding over a house which contains the mummified remains of the foetus, and in which the heroine has become incarcerated. The fact that Aura is one of the film's investigators as well as daughter of the "headhunter" killer reiterates the theme of transgressive familial relations at the core of the narrative.

By frequently casting his daughters within the
macabre fictional world of the *giallo* as well as depicting
violence erupting within and between siblings, Argento has

expressed an interest in the destructive and sexual underside of the family. Central to this examination has been a violent and disturbing construction of the mother who threatens to smother the individuality of the offsprings under her charge.

While Argento's interest in the theme of the destructive maternal agent was most famously demonstrated in the figures of the "three mothers" of **Suspiria** (1977) and **Inferno** (1980), it is also present in earlier productions such as **Profondo Rosso** (1975). Here, the effeminate musician Carlo is revealed as part of a murderous duo, assisting in a series of killings in order to protect the identity of his psychotic mother. More recently, films such as **Trauma, Opera** (1987) and **The Stendhal Syndrome** (1996) have indicated Argento's growing interest in the problematic relations between powerful mothers and their daughters. **Opera** for instance, presents the figure of Betty, whose childhood memories are marked by the scenarios of torture and sadistic coitus organised by her mother and her lover Alan Santini.

Although absent from the narrative of **The Stendhal Syndrome**, the mother of Anna Manni still manages to exert a transgressive influence over this central protagonist. The narrative depicts how Manni's repeated encounters with a serial killer result in her becoming psychotic and reproducing his murderous quest. However, Manni's obsession with art which unites her with her male oppressor is revealed as having been instilled in her by her childhood visits to galleries with her mother.

What interests me in the theme of Argento's murderous mothers (and their daughters) is not merely their homicidal intent, but also their physiological construction which often provokes disgust in both the protagonist and spectator. Frequently, these are female figures whose bodies are either forcibly altered through violent interaction or open to supernatural transformation which indicates physiology as unrestrained. By postulating that Argento's films as well (as other forms of Italian horror) are dominated by images of the disgusting, monstrous female body I shall draw on psychoanalytical theories of gender and identity.

In particular, Julia Kristeva's work around abjection and disgust will be employed to indicate how such images draw on the individual's pre-Oedipal and repressed relations to the maternal agent. I shall argue that the figure of the debased, monstrous and yet potent mother which occupies much of her analysis is also central to the themes of Argento's films.

In her attempt to write back the repressed image of the mother into what she defines as male ordered language and historical structures Kristeva is interested in those aspects which disrupt or disturb the sexuality and identity that the symbolic or the speech act gives us.[2] These fissures or gaps in the self refer back to infancy and the repressed relationship with the maternal agent that dominates these early years. According to her analysis, certain types of artistic representation draw upon the attractions and tensions of early infancy and to the period when the child's (lack of) identity was bound up with its relations with the mother.

Although these early, pleasurable encounters are often repressed when the child gains an understanding of its gender identity within the symbolic, they are never fully restrained. These tensions threaten to re-emerge in later life either through mental trauma, nightmares or "poetic" works of art. According to Kristeva, certain aesthetic strategies and modes of art draw upon the primary bond between mother and child. This is seen both through an obsession with excessive, disgusting, infantile acts, as well as an attempt to dislodge and subvert the dominant structures of language which hold our adult, gendered identity in place. In so doing, these artistic works reference not merely the infant's destructive and archaic early tendencies but also the subversive power of the mother during this primary period of development.

I : IMAGES OF THE MONSTROUS FEMALE BODY IN ITALIAN HORROR

Upon first appearance, issues of female power would not

seem to sit easily with the traditional generic definitions of Argento's work as part of the *giallo* cycle of thrillers that were dominant in Italian cinema during the 1960s and 1970s. This is because films such as **The Bird With The Crystal Plumage** (1970) and **Tenebrae** (1982) were seen by critics as reliant on the voyeuristic depiction of the female body as a site of mutilation. As Mark Le Fanu commented on the release of **Tenebrae**:

*Argento's preoccupation after **Suspiria** seems to be with devising increasingly nasty ways of killing his characters, especially when they are women. Each murder scene occasions a dazzling assemblage of cinematic effects – the camera tracks its victims who gaze back in erotic appreciation of their own vulnerability.*[3]

Although Argento does dwell on the (sexual) suffering of female victims, it is also noticeable that they can also occupy positions of mastery and aggression within his films. This crucial oscillation can be evidenced through characters such as Monica Ranieri and Anna Manni from **The Bird With The Crystal Plumage** and **The Stendhal Syndrome** respectively. In both films their gender identity is altered as a result of violent male assault which in both cases leads them to adopt a sadistic, murderous male quest. By disclosing the identity of killers whose behaviours eschew gender expectations, the resolutions of both films are shocking.

However, the "female" killers they portray are also rendered "disgusting" by virtue of having their bodies forcibly altered and made offensive because of the male violence which induced their psychosis. In **The Bird With The**

Crystal Plumage, Monica's identity crisis is the result of a past genital violation by a male assailant. The repeated violation of Anna Manni at the hands of serial killer Alfredo Grossi results in her having to "reconstruct" her damaged femininity through the aid of artificial cosmetics in order to hide the scars of her ordeal.

Thus, Argento's films use a *giallo* framework to organise narratives around the desire to uncover the identity of a transgressor, while also construct their females as victims of violence or symbolic castration. Paradoxically, they also depict certain female characters who either by adopting the role of the maternal or by virtue of their status as former victims manage to evade this position of oppression. While the existence of these protagonists depicts the construction of aberrant female physiology as a source of disgust, they also indicate these potent characters as being incorporated from other Italian popular genres such as the Peplum (historical adventure film) and the Gothic horror genres of the 1950s.

Traditionally, Italian popular cinema has been seen as a medium marked by a fusion of differing film genres[4] and Carol Jenks has made the link between the *giallo* and other cycles in terms of its depiction of the aberrant female body. Her analysis of the star image of actress Barbara Steele traces her popularity as a Gothic icon in Italian horror films of the 1950s, to a longer tradition depicting fatalistic and monstrous female figures. Steele was frequently cast as a seductive vampire or witch, whose "excessive" desires provoked retribution from assembled male characters in films such as Mario Bava's **The Mask Of The Demon** (1960).

According to Jenks, these characteristics of the provocative but deadly female figure recall the *Divisimo* films of the silent years. These cast actresses such as Theda Bara in roles which drew on historical and mythical depictions of duplicitous and evil women such as Delilah and Cleopatra. While these historical figures remained popular in a series of 1950s Italian historical dramas, they were complemented by the roles undertaken by Steele, most famously in Bava's film. Here she is cast in the role of the witch Asa, who is executed along with her lover Javutich at the beginning of the film. Before being killed (by having a spiked mask forced onto her face), she swears vengeance on her brother and the Vidor family for her torture and execution. Two hundred years later, her rotting corpse is reanimated by the blood of a Victorian surgeon, Kruvajan, who cuts his arm when examining her tomb. Although Asa carries out her threat to destroy the male lineage of the Vidor family, the narrative reveals her real quest to be to inhabit the body and beauty of her identical descendant Katia (also played by Steele). In so doing the film establishes a pattern where subjectivity and identity between opposing female relations become ambivalent:

It becomes clear in the course of the film that good and evil have numerous shared traits, an ambivalence that is neatly visualized by the introduction of the heroine. Princess Katia is essentially the antithesis of the witch, yet the separation is not total ...Her duel role is especially significant; even at this point in her career, Steele was viewed as the ideal dream girl of paranoiacs who imagine hideous menace lurking behind every pretty face.[5]

Asa's attempted fusion with Katia is foregrounded in the finale of **The Mask Of The Demon** when the hero (played by John Richardson) is forced to decide which of the pair is the evil witch who must once again be burned for her transgressions. Although the pair look identical (the witch regaining her former facial beauty from the close proximity with her intended victim), Richardson finally identifies Asa by tearing back her gown to reveal her decaying, insect ridden body. The fact that it is her hideous physiology that reveals the witch's true status is important, as it reiterates the construction of the feminine in these cycles as monstrous. This difficulty in

locating Asa's body that **The Mask Of The Demon** highlights, provided a template for later roles that Steele adopted. In Antonio Margheriti's **The Long Hair Of Death** (1964) Jenks notes that she is also cast as a witch who only reveals her filthy decaying body to her lover after they have engaged in sexual intercourse.

Argento's work has attempted to translate these Gothic concerns around the transformative and monstrous nature of the female body into the investigative framework of the *giallo*. The impact of these two film modes on his work is clearly seen in the film **Demons**, which he produced in 1985. This film was directed by Lamberto Bava (son of Mario), and openly traces the importance of **The Mask Of The Demon** on contemporary Italian horror film culture. This set of self-reflexive references is achieved by staging the film's action in a disused cinema, where an invited audience is attacked by possessed patrons while watching an untitled horror film. Among the assembled viewers are a blind man Werner and his female assistant Liz. Their casting refers back to the *giallo*, and to Argento's interest in blind detectives such as Franco Arno in **The Cat O'Nine Tails** (1971). The cinema features other references to Argento's work, with posters for **Four Flies On Grey Velvet** (1971) and George A. Romero's 1978 film **Dawn Of The Dead** (for which Argento wrote the screenplay) being displayed in the theatre foyer.

However, with its emphasis on the visible aspects of the transformative female body, **Demons** also casts clear references to the earlier Italian Gothic horror traditions of the 1950s and 1960s. For instance, the trigger for the chaos that engulfs the theatre is a cursed display mask hanging in the cinema foyer. The mask is identical to the one forced over

Barbara Steele's face in **The Mask Of The Demon**. Importantly, the first patrons to be infected are two black prostitutes Rosemary and Candy who don the mask before entry to the screening. Their coding as explicit sites of erotic visual display also draws equations with the paradoxes apparent in Barbara Steele's star image. While both the **Demons** characters are depicted as signifiers of sexual attraction, their bodies are marked by a sudden degeneration into decay and death, comparable to that of Asa from Mario Bava's film.

Demons even parodies the duality between Asa and Katia established in **The Mask Of The Demon** through its casting of Natasha Hovey as the central female protagonist

Cheryl. Although described by Rob Winning as a "symbol of all that is innocent and unblemished in the world"[6], Cheryl unsettles the clarity of this definition. During the film's closing sequence, her body suddenly transforms in to a demon. This act is both horrific (in terms of the intensity of transformation depicted) and unsettling, revealing that the viewer's stable source of identification throughout the narrative has been infected all the time.

While examples from both **The Mask Of The Demon** and **Demons** indicate a shared cinematic history, their depiction of an uncontrollable female physiology link them to the processes of disgust and abjection defined by Kristeva. Their bodies reveal defiance of the symbolic's regulation and discipline over physiology, and thus recall an earlier period, prior to the processes of separation between the mother and infant. This imaginary dyad is fragmented as a consequence of the discovery of sexual difference and the threat of castration which defines the child's absorption into the symbolic. It is the child's interpellation into the language system which works to fragment the former ambivalences around its identity and gender.

However, what Argento's narratives do is draw attention to the artificial processes of language itself. By constructing bodies of disgust, paradox and excess the feminine of the *giallo* indicates the ease with which physiology can be dislocated from the terms, polarities and categorisations that discourse constructs. Specifically, Argento's horrific females, by virtue of their impossible construction, foreground the importance of the border in cultural and linguistic systems of classification.

The importance of the "border" as a system of cultural

classification has been noted by Mary Douglas's research on ritual communities. Here it is used to initiate common bonds of identification across clan members, legitimising of certain sexual relations, via a capacity to "externalise" outsiders. Such methods, though central to these groups' survival are subject to a series of potential "physiological" disruptions which must be recuperated within the existing system of classification.

Thus, in the Hindu caste system, the position of the privileged Brahmin subset is undercut by waste matter such as excreta, urine, saliva and menstruational blood. These emissions not only undercut the definition of what constitutes the external appearance of the body, but are also functions attributable to all castes. This potential for the body's transgression is recuperated in this system by the Coorgs, whose social status as "dirt" is confirmed by their responsibility for the disposal of such waste matter, as well as the preparation of the dead.

It is the symbolic's attempt to resurrect and maintain the self as clean and ordered that is also central to Julia Kristeva's account of abjection. In the book *Powers Of Horror*, she defines abjection as an erosion of the borders of subjectivity which can be explored from a psychoanalytical perspective. The child's identity is formed through its absorption into a system of language which is itself dependant on the polarization of self, sexuality and external body image into a series of discrete binaries and categories. These terms:

...need to be oppositionally coded in order for the child's body to be constituted as a unified whole and for its subjectivity to be defined and tied to the body's limits. They are conditions

*under which the child may claim the body as its own, and thus
also the conditions under which it gains a place as a speaking
subject.[7]*

Central to the functioning of this system of subjectivity is the
repression of the infant's pre-linguistic fascination with its
own body and its associated waste products. Here, Kristeva
draws on Douglas's definition of the body's waste products as
a troubling type of "dirt", marked by matter such as faeces,
urine, vomit, spittle and menstrual blood. These body
products are seen as "taboo" because they operate and
intersect at the space between the interior of the self and its
external image. As a result, they deny crucial borders through
which the symbolic attempts to construct "the clean and
proper body."[8]

Although Kristeva argues that despite the symbolic
attempts to banish these forms of primary pleasure, they
recur in later life either through psychological disorders or
unconventional works of art. Kristeva draws similar
conclusions to Lacan's work on psychosis, highlighting the
ability of such disorders to rob the subject of the security
which surrounds the perception of an established body
image. Equally, her conclusion that the abject occurs through
certain unconventional works of art is replicated by both the
content and form of Argento's cinema.

Central to many of his films is the displacement of the
border and the mechanisms of symbolic clarification that they
represent. For instance, bodily matter such as blood and
mucus proves central to the source of infection that marks the
Metropol cinema in **Demons**. Here, it is Candy's blood that
initiates infection when she is scratched by the cursed display

mask in the theatre. As a result, her external body image displays a lack of integrity and control by erupting in to a series of facial lesions, which eventually burst, sending a shower of blood and green pus cascading down her neck.

As with the construction of waste matter in Kristeva's analysis, the eruption of these bodies in **Demons** provokes disgust because it undercuts the established boundaries of external appearance. In the case of Candy, this corporeal "corruption" is marked by the "shedding" of her established form: her fingernails and teeth being replaced by claws and a phallic shaped tongue. According to Barbara Creed's book *The Monstrous Feminine* it is the corruption of established body and identity boundaries which remains at the core of the horror film's paradoxical appeal through disgust. Adapting what she identifies as key borders transgressed in horror cinema, it can be argued that Argento's work is also concerned with the elision of the boundary between the human and unhuman (as in **Demons**, **Inferno**, **Suspiria** and **Phenomena** [1985]), as well as the boundary separating established gender distinctions (**The Bird With The Crystal Plumage** and **Profondo Rosso**).

II : FILTH, FOOD, SEXUALITY AND THE MOTHER: CATEGORIES OF THE ABJECT

Despite the difference in the above type or category of abjection, in each case Argento concentrates on the female body as a signifier of disgust and chaotic transformation. Although **Demons** details a process of physical possession afflicting both sexes, it is interesting to note that the narrative does not visualize the male body undergoing the same excessive transmutations afflicting depicted female characters. One reason behind this preoccupation links these images back to infancy and in particular the young child's initial relations with its mother.

Prior to the discovery of its own autonomy the infant's dependence on the mother is indicated in her primary role in the training, coordinating and controlling of its body. Her role is particularly marked through the supervised expulsion and disposal of waste matter such as urine and excreta. Kristeva defines this process of maternal control over the infant's body as a process of "primary mapping". This includes activities such as sphincteral training which allows the child to discover the contours of his own developing body, while retaining the gratification of contact with the mother's form (through activities such as breast feeding).

As a result of her close proximity to these sources of waste matter, the mother becomes viewed as "abject by association" by the child when it enters the symbolic. Although her influence in this primary period of physical development is repressed, it returns as a sight of horror and disgust in the unpalatable representations of the female body in Italian horror cinema. These figures display an inability to control bodily hygiene, an association with images of mucus and filth that confirms bodily matter as a key form of abjection.

This capacity for waste matter to invoke this primary maternal bond is indicated in Kristeva's example of "A". This case study detailed the actions of a four-year-old child whose recurrent nightmare focused on his attempted expulsion of faeces.[9] When the substance was emitted, it refused to be detached from "A"'s body, and in fact transformed into a monster, which the child defined as a cross between a frog and a crocodile. The threat that the monster offers, is as a disruption to the unity of the external body image, and its links to symbolic regulation. Whereas the established image of the self offers the individual a guarantor of distinct identity, faecal matter is marked by "the mixtures, alterations and decay"[10] that run counter to such modes of classification. Importantly, the nightmare that plagued the child coincided with his emerging understanding of the rules that govern modes of verbal communication. The dream thus reveals a slippage between two developmental registers: the past realm of the mother, the body and its waste products and the symbolic with its attempted repression of these former contacts and modes of gratification.

The fact that "A"'s nightmare evokes a period prior to his construction as a subject is intimated by the entrance of the father into the narrative; the dream ending when he "sees the animal and threatens punishment."[11] Indeed, given that the monster which attached itself to "A"'s anus possessed a transparent membrane, it is worth remembering that in **Demons**, during her transformation, Candy's face is transformed by a network of blood vessels rising from the interior of her body to corrupt its external appearance.

While waste matter remains one of the key types of abjection that Kristeva identifies, other variants such as food loathing and the obliteration of the signs of sexual difference are also furnished by Argento's works. According to Kristeva, food loathing is "perhaps the most elementary and archaic form of abjection"[12]. As she notes in *Powers Of Horror*, such loathing is of particular importance in the renunciation of this maternal bond. Not only does it evoke the primary "oral" period of infantile dependence, but it also undercuts the role of distinction cultural categorization. Kristeva exemplifies the notion of food loathing and the cultural borders it disturbs with the example of the skin that forms on fetid milk. This provokes disgust not only because of its smell, but also as it conflates the distinction of the food matter as *either* solid or liquid, eroding the border "between two distinct entities or territories"[13]. Evidence of food loathing is provided in Argento films such as **Suspiria**. Here, meat is rendered unfit for human consumption through an infestation by maggots. It is also linked to a plague of rats in the film's sequel **Inferno**.[14]

What is important about both **Suspiria** and **Inferno** is that abject waste matter is clearly equated with the maternal through the narrative concentration on a trio of witches called "the three mothers". These destructive figures are revealed to dominate the world and spread pestilence via a series of cursed locations in Rome, New York and Freiburg. **Suspiria** explores this destructive maternal presence by concentrating on the activities of Mater Suspiriorum, who hides under the guise of Helena Marcos, the head of a dance school in Germany.

The film shows that this witch and her female assistants work to infantilise those in close proximity with them. **Suspiria** depicts the school as dominated by a series of destructive female figures, in particular Miss Tanner, a dance instructor, and Madame Blanc, the key principal of the institution. Importantly, Argento makes these two figures the focus for a series of masculine figures who are dependant on them as maternal substitutes. For instance, Madame Blanc is constantly accompanied by her nephew Albert, a young child upon whom she directs all her affection.[15] This relationship is in turn mirrored by Miss Tanner's fondness for a young (and

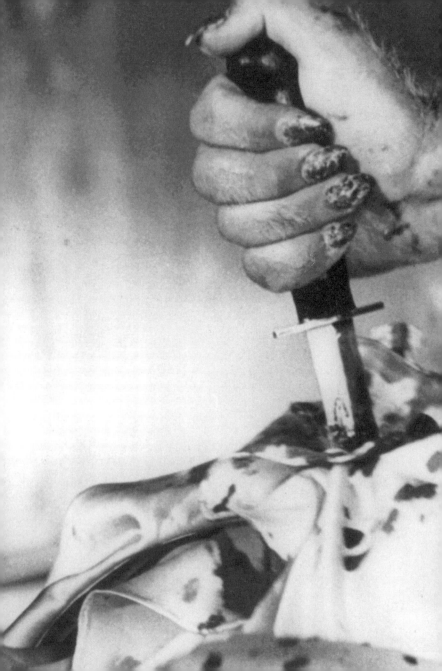

destitute) male dancer whom she allows to stay on at the academy despite his inability to pay the fees. Even the academy pianist is rendered dependant on these female agents (as guides) by virtue of his being blind.

What **Suspiria** points to is an absence of controlling male figures, allowing these maternal figures to limit the autonomy of the individuals under their charge. The film reveals that they violently dispatch those who discover their true identity. The inspiration for **Suspiria** can be partly traced to the experiences of Argento's former partner and long term collaborator Dario Nicolodi at a ballet school during her youth. Although Nicolodi moulded rumours that the institution was ruled by witches into a screen play for the film, it was Argento who constructed these figures as destructive maternal agents. As he stated:

...in an early draft I even planned to have the action take place in a school where the witches were teachers who tortured the children.[16]

According to Leon Hunt's article "A (Sadistic) Night At The Opera", further sources of inspiration for **Suspiria** and **Inferno** are Thomas De Quincy's essay *Levana And Our Ladies Of Sorrow*[17], as well as earlier Italian Gothic narratives popularised by the 1960s works of Mario Bava and Antonio Margheriti. As a result, they appear to differ from the *giallo* framework that characterises other Argento texts. However, despite the supernatural emphasis to both films, they retain the investigative quest that defines other Argento works. In **Suspiria**, the lead female protagonist Susy Bannion assumes the role of investigator in order to discover the truth behind

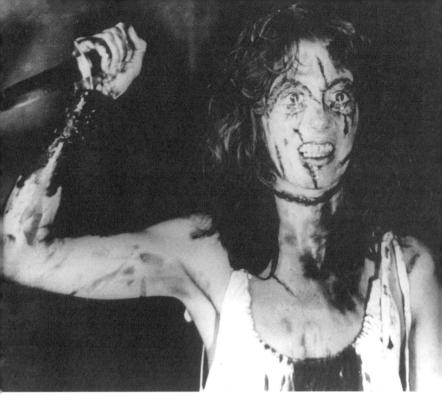

the disappearance of her friends at the school. In the film's sequel, **Inferno**, the role of detective is taken be Mark Elliot, whose sister Rose discovers one of the witches living in a New York apartment. Rose is subsequently killed for gaining this knowledge about the mothers, resulting in Mark's journey to the hotel to investigate her disappearance.

Both films (reiterating Argento's statement) construct the three mothers as cruel, duplicitous and threatening. These traits can be once more be linked to Kristeva's theory of abjection. She argues that upon entry into the symbolic, the infant renounces the mother as a figure of erotic attraction.

While the functioning of the symbolic relies the clean, ordered and categorised body, the repressed dyad points back "to that time when the mother-child relationship was marked by an untrammelled pleasure in 'playing' with the body and its wastes."[18] However, this process of repression is frequently disturbed by mothers who refuse to allow their children independence.

In such cases, the infant becomes trapped between the two developmental registers: the initial mode of maternal dependence (which she terms the semiotic) and the later stage of identity and language acquisition implicit in the symbolic. As a result of this split, the mother becomes recast from a nurturing to a threatening figure, who works to limit the autonomy of her offspring. In *The Monstrous Feminine*, Creed pinpoints the long tradition that the horror genre has of constructing such destructive maternal figures. For instance, she pinpoints the characters of Mrs Bates from Hitchcock's **Psycho** (1960) and Mrs White from De Palma's **Carrie** (1977) as two examples of maternal agents who restrain the autonomy of their children. In these works:

...the maternal figure is constructed as the monstrous feminine. By refusing to relinquish her hold on her child, she prevents it from taking up its proper place in relation to the symbolic. Partly consumed by the desire to remain locked in a blissful relationship with the mother and partly terrified of separation, the child finds it easy to succumb to the comforting pleasure of the dyadic relationship.[19]

It is this threatening construction of the maternal which frames Argento's **Inferno**. Here, the status of the three

mothers as an abject and threatening presence is established
in the pre-credit sequence, when a voice over (revealed to be
that of an architect named Varelli) narrates how he designed
three dwelling places for the witches. His reference that these
locations have become the "repository of all their *filthy*
secrets" establishes an equation between the maternal and
abject waste matter in the narrative.

Inferno reveals a New York hotel to be the home of
another of the trio: Mater Tenebrarum. As well as being
plagued by rats, the location is also revealed as having a
sickening stench which disgusts those inhabitants in close
proximity to the site. Indeed, Varelli's voice over which opens
the film comments that the deathly "reek" of the mother's
dwelling place acts as a "primary key" to their foul presence.
This reference locates the maternal realm at the level of

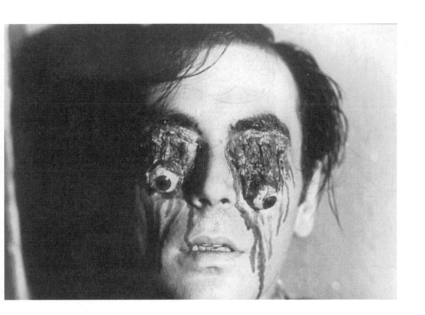

physiology and corporeal mapping, and (as the narrative reveals), beyond the limits of discourse. The film's opening sequence depicts the film's ill-fated heroine Rose Elliot exploring the caverns of the New York hotel after reading Varelli's writings. These underground locations, which remain submerged in water instantly connote the maternal through a womb-like structure. However, the film instantly introduces a tension into the traditional equation of the maternal with the fertile by having Rose's exploration disturbed by her discovery of skeletons and abject body bits in the underground location. This recasting of the womb as a site of death rather than the source of creation confirms Varelli's initial statement of the witches as barren mothers who are "incapable of creating life"[20].

Importantly, the significance of a hidden chamber or

secret room which contains a site of death and decay is
central to several key Argento texts. While **Inferno**'s
submerged cellar holds the key to Mater Tenebrarum's
identity, her counterpart from **Suspiria** is concealed in a
secret room whose passages are lined with the dead bodies of
her victims from the dance academy. In these locations the
monstrous mother "commits dreadful acts in a location which
resembles the womb. These inter-uterine settings consist of
dark, narrow winding passages leading to a central room,
cellar or symbolic place of birth."[21] The fact that these
locations are so often the sites of death and decay in
Argento's works can also be linked to Kristeva's analysis of

waste matter, abjection and the dissolution of identity. In *Powers Of Horror*, she identifies key examples of waste matter as menstruational and excremental. Not only do these fragment the border dividing interior and exterior divisions of the body, but they also refer to the womb and the mother's reproductive abilities. While the mother's fertility is referenced by the menstruational cycle, the actual birth act is also connoted through the (often violent) expulsion of excremental and decaying substance.

It is these images of blood and violent birth that Argento's film's and the earlier Italian horror cycles play upon. For instance, evidence of the abject construction of the womb in Gothic horror works such as **The Mask Of The Demon**. Here, the witch Asa assumes the role of "barren" mother by resurrecting her dead lover Javutich from a deserted graveyard. This sequence appears as if a parody of birth, with the male figure emerging from "the erupting earth, his hands covered with a web of mucus"[22]. A similar equation of the womb as a site of death and decaying bodily waste is evidenced in **Demons**, (once more demonstrating Argento's wish to comment on the importance of Mario Bava's film). Here, one of the film's key protagonists Cathy, experiences a bizarre version of the birth act when a demon literally *tears* through the surface of her skin following a process of unnoticed internal incubation. According to Kristeva, in such images the:

...evocation of the maternal body and childbirth induces the image of birth as a violent act of expulsion through which the nascent body tears itself away from the maternal insides.[23]

While depictions of the grotesque female body and the birth act provide a clear link between **Demons** and Bava's work, a direct comparison can also be found between **The Mask Of The Demon** and **Inferno**. This is seen in the fact that Mario Bava worked on the latter in the capacity of special effects designer (his son Lamberto also featured as an assistant director on the production). Bava's role in **Inferno** included the creation of the underwater cavern that Rose Elliot discovers prior to her disappearance.

Importantly, the only represented reference to the mothers during this sequence, is a painting of Mater Tenebrarum which hangs in the underground cavern that Rose Elliot explores. However, confirming Kristeva's conclusion that the female form cannot fully be represented by a male ordered language, it appears pertinent that only the *name* rather than the image of the mother is presented in the

painting. This feature is itself important as it points to another type of abjection that Argento's mothers share: the ability to upset or transcend an established body image and the signs of sexual difference.

The mothers prove to be female characters whose presence undercuts external and internal categorisations of the body, once more reflecting the primary ambivalence that surrounds the infant's sense of self. For instance, Mater Suspiriorum exists in **Suspiria** as a force without either shape or distinction[24], only being locatable by her breathing (which, in sounding like a death rattle reiterates her body as a site of decay). Importantly, the film's heroine Suzy manages to destroy the witch by identifying the shadow of her outline in a thunderstorm. When in death Suspiriorum does materialise (revealing herself to be an aged hag) her body is once more coded as a site of "dead" flesh.

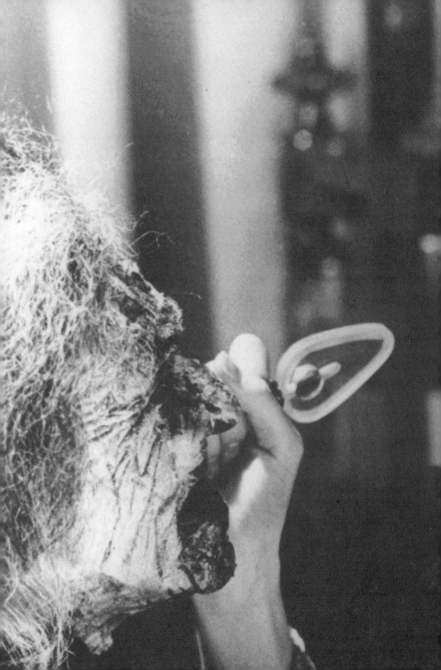

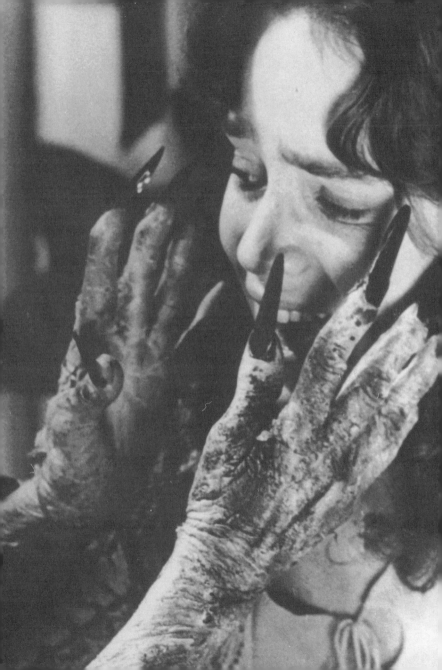

This ability to defy symbolic codes of physiological representation is also present in the closing sequence of **Inferno**. Here, the hero Mark Elliot discovers the lair of one of the witches after investigating the disappearance of his sister Rose at Mater Tenebrarum's New York apartment block. His actions set in motion a blaze at the building, in which he discovers that Mater Tenebrarum is actually a nurse who tends for the (now mute and disabled) architect Varelli. While recapitulating the reduction of the male to infantile status initiated in **Suspiria**, Tenebrarum's unholy power is also indicated in her sudden transformation from human into skeletal form as she chases Elliot through the blazing building[25]. This apparent ability to defy the stability of categorical representation fits well with the conception of the mother as a dominant and feared figure whom (the infant often fantasizes) is able to transcend the borders of her own form. The trauma that this imagined ability for transformation provokes in the subject's sense of self seems recapitulated in the film's ending via the fear induced in Elliot when Tenebrarum states his own body will undergo a series of changes under her power.

Mater Tenebrarum's transformation in **Inferno**'s finale indicates the transience of the barrier between the ordered exterior of the body and its underlying physiology. More important, by appearing as a figure of death she draws attention to Kristeva's definition of the corpse as "the ultimate abjection". Her conclusion that death ejects the self from the body shell is echoed by Douglas who finds the corpse as governed by a duel process of decay, initially retaining the external features which defined its former identity, before this "pseudo identity" is itself replaced by a drive towards ultimate decay.

III : FROM THE MONSTROUS MOTHER TO THE "THIRD SEX"

What is also evidenced by the corpse is the displacement of the centrality of the symbolic's drive towards sexual definition. Here, in the absence of distinct identity, any concept of biological difference is replaced with the notion of the body as "flesh". Beyond **Suspiria** and **Inferno**, several other key Argento's films figure the human form reduced to as series of body "bits" under the influence of the abject and monstrous mother. For instance, this construction is clearly marked in **Phenomena**, in a narrative which deals with a cannibalistic serial killer whom stalks a Swiss border town community. The only clues that the police have to trace the murderer are the series of pieces of discarded flesh left at the scene of each crime. As with **Suspiria**, the key to the identity

of the assassin is revealed to be contained in a dance school once more populated with aggressive female teachers.

The film's heroine Jennifer Corvino discovers the killer to be the deformed child harboured by her school headmistress Mrs Bruckner. The film depicts the dyad between Bruckner and her child as a mutual preoccupation with the flesh. This is indicated in the closing sequence of the film. Jennifer, trapped in the secret caverns of Bruckner's home (again reflecting an abject depiction of the womb) falls into a vat containing the decaying limbs of the victims that the killer has been collecting. In his review of the film, John Martin has noted the film's preoccupation with abjection, commenting that:

...the killer is inextricably bound up in the world of the flesh, to the extent of surrounding himself/herself with human remains, and is eventually revealed as a cleft-headed mutant... Conceived in an act of brutal rape and itself a necrophile, the monster testifies to an overpowering disgust with the whole process of procreation...[26]

As Martin notes, the gender of the monstrous child remains ambivalent, a feature which once again recalls the elision of the boundaries of sexuality through abjection. Importantly, this denial of difference is replicated by Bruckner's own body which is revealed to have been mutilated in the rape that impregnated her. This attack occurred when a mental patient under her charge pulled her through the bars of his cell, disfiguring her breasts in the process. As a result, Bruckner is left with a "damaged" body that can no longer fully be classified as feminine. This concentration on the damaged female body that denies biological classifications can be seen as consistent trope in Argento's films.

Thus, Bruckner's deformity is matched by Monica Ranieri's genital violation in **The Bird With The Crystal Plumage**. Here, the painting that leads amateur detective Sam Dalmas to uncover the killer's identity (depicting a woman being genitally penetrated by an assailant's knife), is revealed to a representation of the attack Ranieri suffered and then used as a psychotic template to assault other young women.[27] This act of "feminine" mutilation itself prefigures the fate of Adriana Petrescu, the psychic "headhunter" killer from Argento's later film **Trauma**. Here, her vagina is penetrated with a surgeon's knife while she is giving birth. This act not only alters her own genital appearance but decapitates her baby, resulting in her quest to exact vengeance on the malpractice which aborted her pregnancy.[28]

As with **Phenomena**, **Trauma** provides a point of comparison to the narrative of the "three mothers" by constructing the maternal as a mutilated deviation from symbolic boundaries of categorisation. A comparison with the "dead" womb of Mater Tenebrarum's hotel basement is replicated by Petrescu's damaged reproductive organs, while Adriana is also cast as the powerful pre-Oedipal mother who threatens to smother her daughter Aura's autonomy.[29] As a result, Aura comes to attain a complex position in relation to the investigative processes of the film. Believing her mother's powers as a medium have resulted in her assassination by a killer fearful of exposure, Aura teams up with David Parson, a typical example of Argento's amateur male detectives. As with other masculine investigators from the cycle, Parson is shown to lack the symbolic mandate needed to resolve the enigma of the killer's identity. His close proximity to the case is revealed through his role as a design artist in the television studio covering the head hunter killings.[30] Parson is separated from an appropriate position of knowledge needed to resolve the crime. This is indicated through his inability to make accurate visual deductions about the killer's identity (whom he believes is Aura's male psychiatrist Dr Judd).

An indication of this visual inability to read a scene for "evidence" is provided not only through Parson's misguided belief that the killer is male, but that Aura, like her

mother is a passive potential victim. This belief is marked in the opening sequence when David manages to save Aura from drowning, agreeing to help her through a belief that she is unbalanced. Later in the film, Parson discovers that Aura is anorexic after she confesses that she is unable to have

intercourse with him.[31] Soon after this revelation he receives a note from her stating that she has "gone to join her mother", leading him to presume that she has committed suicide while in an unbalanced frame of mind.

As a result, he falls into a state of a psychosis and begins to wander the streets, endlessly mistaking other women for his lost love object. It is only in the closing stages of the film when Parson finds Aura alive and living with her aggressive murderous mother that his perceptions equating passivity and femininity are unhinged.

Indeed, Aura's anorexia, the disorder which confirmed Parson's view of her passivity can in fact be re-read as a sign of her resisting a stable form of sexual identity.[32] As a result of this disorder, Aura's relation with the abject is doubly coded. Firstly, her mother's transgressions take the form of decapitating and then dissecting the bodies of her victims. Equally, her own anorexia recalls food loathing as a fundamental form of abjection related to the infant's primary period of development under the mother.

Louise J. Kaplan has linked disorders such as anorexia nervosa to the concept of "maternal perversity"[33], arguing that the complaint is actually the extension of the dyad that marked the infant's relation to its mother. In the book *Female Perversions* she notes the disorder to be marked in patients who feel unable to transcend the control of the pre-Oedipal mother despite being caught up in the symbolic's mode of sexual classification. The girl's response to this contradictory situation is (through a denial of food) to attempt to refuse any external signs of sexual difference. She thus attempts a return to a primary state of semiotic fusion which discards gender difference.[34] In this respect, it is important that Kaplan has found the disease to be marked in those girls who recall having powerful, maternal figures in their lives.

Kaplan has noted the historical emergence of the disorder in relation to 19th century medical and aesthetic discourses around femininity. However, rather than see it as a sign of female passivity, she argues anorexia represents a form of physiological resistance to the symbolic. As a result, the anorexic can be seen as another instance of the diseased female that provoked disgust in Freud's dream. Their diseased body provokes offence in those males who are in close proximity to them. What the sufferer attempts to do in this condition is return to an arena which denies the notion of sexual difference and the mother's body as lacking. (As Kaplan noted in *Female Perversions,* it is important that the disorder only emerges in a girl's teenage years when her mature sexual identity is becoming marked).[35]

Although the anorexic appears to be defined as a passive, genderless child, Kaplan argues that this desire to become the "third sex" demonstrates the female's possession of aggressive pre-Oedipal instincts. As one sufferer indicated, the desired effect for physiological transformation was only deemed successful in the advanced stages of the disorder. Here, she was no longer able to menstruate, and hormonal imbalances had produced the growth of facial hair:

I got my wish to be a third sex, both girl and boy. Standing in front of the mirror. I saw a lovely attractive woman. My other self, the body outside the mirror, was a lusting young man preparing to seduce the girl in the mirror. I was having a love affair with myself.[36]

The anorexic's ultimate aim is the regression to a realm where sexual difference and the law of the father are denied. It is this wish that is reciprocated in the ending of **Trauma**. Here, Aura is revealed to have literally returned to a primary arena of the maternal. Parson discovers her (in an advanced anorexic state) and Adriana living in a house which contains the mummified remains of the aborted infant that initiated the mother's quest. Although Adriana the monstrous mother of the text is destroyed in the film's finale, the questions over her daughter's ambivalent sexuality remain unresolved. The film ends with her having to be helped from the scene by Parson.

Indeed, during the end credit sequence, the camera shifts away from the couple, pans across the street and comes to rest on a young girl who is dancing in a window. Although this action has no apparent diegetic motivation, the young girl's body is as asexual and prepubescent as Aura's. As with Argento's other films, this seems to confirm that the text's "troublesome" construction of the female body exceeds simplistic generic definitions as a victimised, mutilated form. Rather, it represents a disturbing, potent and unclassifiable body that resists ideological recouperation even in the closing stages of his films.

NOTES

1. Dario Argento, quoted in David E. Williams' article "Argento's Enigma", *Film Threat* #8, Volume 2, February 1993, p.44.

2. Kristeva's interests in language, ideology and the representation of the feminine are split along a number of important publications which chart the formation of her ideas on the repression of the maternal in patriarchal society. Texts such as *Revolution In Poetic Language* (New York: Columbia University Press, 1984) provide an examination of the strict, rule bound systems of language that govern the symbolic, while contrasting them to the fluid forms of communication which exist between the mother and child. Both this volume and *Powers Of Horror* (New York: Columbia University Press, 1982) indicate how subversive forms of discourse used between the pair reappear in certain forms of modernist literature. Although cinema remains largely absent from her analysis, it is the examination of the mother as a sign of symbolic disgust and loathing within these texts that resulted in critics such as Barbara Creed applying Kristeva's work to the horror film. More recently, volumes such as *Tales Of Love* (New York: Columbia University Press, 1987) have shown Kristeva attempting to write accounts of the history of motherhood using unconventional and subversive written techniques. These methods are present in chapters such as "Stabat Mater" in order to show how an "infantile" use of discourse can be used to represent the feminine in language.

3. Mark Le Fanu, "Tenebrae" in *Films And Filming* #348, September 1983, p.36.

4. See Christopher Wagstaff's "A Forkful Of Westerns", in Richard Dyer & Ginette Vincendeau (eds) *Popular European Cinema*, London: Routledge, 1992. Here, Wagstaff has sought to give historical reasons for the dominance of the generic hybrid in post-war Italian popular film. He linked the phenomenon to an attempt to appeal to regionally

distinct audiences on the part of producers and filmmakers. Drawing on the geographical distinction between the industrial, "sophisticated" North and the rural South Wagstaff has argued that these distinct locations are marked by differing audience tastes in terms of narrative type and generic mode of engagement. While one specific film cycle may be popular in the sophisticated areas of the country, this appeal may not be matched in rural locations. Thus, by fusing a number of different generic concerns into a single narrative format, producers ensure a market for the film in all areas of the country. Another important account in this area is Leon Hunt's influential article "A Sadistic Night At The Opera: Notes On The Italian Horror Film" (*The Velvet Light Trap* #30, 1992). Here, Hunt situates the Italian horror film between other Italian cycles dominant in post-war years. As a result, he argues that critics often fail to recognise that the curious construction of these narratives does not necessarily represent deficiencies on the part of the director and their knowledge of plotting and film technique. Rather these texts are very self-conscious attempts to appeal to the *specific* interests of these different Italian viewing groups.

5. David J. Hogan, *Dark Romance*, Northampton: Equation, 1988, p.168.

6. Rob Winning, "Demons" in *Cinefantastique* Volume 17 #2, March 1987, p.44.

7. Elizabeth Grosz, "The Body Of Signification" in John Fletcher & Andrew Benjamin (eds) *Abjection Melancholia And Love: The Work Of Julia Kristeva*, London: Routledge, 1996, p.86.

8. Barbara Creed, *The Monstrous Feminine*, London: Routledge, 1994, p.11.

9. In her article "Ellipses On Dread And The Specular Seduction" in *Wide Angle* Volume 3 #2, 1979.

10. Kristeva, *Powers Of Horror*, p.108.

11. Kristeva, "Ellipses On Dread And The Specular Seduction", p.45. It seems pertinent that the narrative does not specify to whom the punishment will be directed: the monster for its sudden appearance, or the infant for creating such a figure from its own "filth".

12. Kristeva, *Powers Of Horror*, p.2.

13. Ibid., p.9. The basis of food loathing is also indicated in Douglas's book *Purity And Danger*, London: Routledge, 1991. This book analysed the rationale behind the construction of certain animals as taboo in religious or ritual practice. In orthodox Judaism only animals whose characteristics equate with the category of their appropriate environment are seen as fit for consumption. Thus, the snake is seen as taboo from this schema because it can inhabit both land and water despite possessing neither gills nor legs and as such defies the distinguishing categories between land animals and fish.

14. This connection is made by Creed in *The Monstrous Feminine* (p.76–77). Her analysis of both Argento's films is tied to the cultural history of representing the female witch as a filthy, unclean presence.

15. Importantly, the boy (aged around seven or eight years old) is clothed in mock Victorian dress more suited to a much younger child. This factor, along with Albert's apparent inability (or refusal) to enter into conversation in the film, redoubles the relationship of the mother to the Pre-Oedipal and pre-articulate child.

16. Maitland McDonagh, *Broken Mirrors Broken Minds: The Dark Dreams Of Dario Argento*, London: Sun Tavern Fields, 1991, p.129.

17. His essay itself privileges uncontrollable physiology, linking the mother's presence as "functions pointing to the flesh". Cited in McDonagh, p.136.

18. Creed, p.13.

19. Ibid., p.12.

20. Ibid., p.77.

21. Ibid., p.53.

22. Jenks, in Richard Dyer & Ginette Vincendeau (eds) *Popular European Cinema*, p.157.

23. Kristeva, *Powers Of Horror*, p.101.

24. Comparisons with Creed's analysis of Mrs Bates from **Psycho** are important here. As she notes this maternal figure operates through the power of the semiotic: she is literally the disembodied "voice", who can only be represented in terms of the "flesh" of a dead corpse. Equally, the body that is revealed as belonging to Mrs Bates in the film's conclusion is marked by a collapse of external image onto "internal" features such as bone structure.

25. Her transformation from the guise of nurse to a "genderless" skeleton reiterates the division of the interior and exterior modes of physiology that abjection attacks.

26. John Martin, in Pierre Jouis (ed) *Fantasy Film Memory: Directed By Dario Argento*, Paris: Gothic Press, 1991, p.42.

27. It is possible to argue that the theme of the "damaged" female body as a trigger for violent psychosis represents a trait in Italian horror beyond Argento's productions. For instance, in his review of Sergio Pastore's **The Crimes Of The Black Cat** (1972), Mark Ashworth links a series of savage murders occurring at a fashion house to an earlier accident suffered by the killer Francoise Balli. See his review of the film in Stephen Thrower (ed) *Eye Ball: The European Sex And Horror Review* #1, Autumn 1989. In Pastore's film, after her breasts and abdomen are disfigured in a car crash, Balli begins to mutilate other females in order to avenge the loss of her own feminine figure. Another example can be found in Aldo Lado's 1975 film **Late Night Trains**. This features Macha Meril as a sadistic businesswomen who goads a pair of thugs into raping and killing two young girls on a trans-European train. Following Monica Ranieri's example Meril kills one of the victims by penetrating her vagina with a knife, to the disgust of her two male assistants. When pressed by

them as to the motivation behind these extreme actions, Meril replies that her own body was similarly deformed by a surgeon's knife during puberty.

28. The construction of the "mutilated" female heroine as a repeated Argento trait is confirmed in the figure Anna Manni from **The Stendhal Syndrome**. Following the repeated wounding on her body by Alfredo Grossi, she experiences a "psychotic" loss of gender identity. As a result she attempts to remodify her image by cutting off her hair and practising body building in order to achieve a more masculine appearance. The dislocation of her body from dominant notions of sexual difference is evidenced in an alteration of Anna's sexual habits. She confesses a hatred of being penetrated during intercourse, even gesturing towards the anal rape of her boyfriend Marco during a lovemaking scene.

29. The casting of Piper Laurie for this role is pertinent. She is most famous for playing the sadistic Mrs White who denies her daughter autonomy in Brian De Palma's **Carrie** (1977). However, as Martin Coxhead has noted, Adriana's construction (both her hair colouring and death at the hand of her own decapitating machine) link her to previous Argento mothers such as Martha from **Profondo Rosso**. See Coxhead's article "Traumatised" in Allan Bryce (ed) *The Dark Side*, April 1994.

30. This redoubles the obsession with replaying visual scenarios of death that marked the similarity between investigator Sam Dalmas and Monica Ranieri in **The Bird With The Crystal Plumage**.

31. Aura's inability to fully adopt a feminine role for the purposes of intercourse mirror the behaviour of Betty in **Opera**. Her access to her mother's past crimes prevents her from developing a mature sexuality, indicated in her inability to engage in intercourse with a young stage hand.

32. Argento consistently retards his heroines' sexuality in the same

way that Aura's disorder prevents her taking up a fully feminine position. Indeed, when asked about his ideal of "female" beauty by Phillip Nutman Argento explained his choice through the figure of Jennifer Corvino from **Phenomena**. Here, Argento stated, "In my opinion she is an angelic vision of womanhood... Her face and form are really powerful, and she's almost sexless." See Nutman's review of **Phenomena** in Anthony Timpone (ed) *Fangoria* #49, November 1985, p.54.

33. In the book *Female Perversions*, p.410.

34. From a Kristevan perspective it can be argued that the anorexic's body can be viewed as a site of abjection on a number of levels. The body becomes a shapeless body shell, thus undercutting existing categorisations of what constitutes established body image. Equally, the ingestion of food becomes impossible: the patient is forced to expel the substances reiterating the inability to control one's own physiology that marked the fate of victims in **Demons**. Recalling Creed's definition of the abject in horror cinema as a site of grotesque spectacle and display, Kaplan notes that through the excessive remoulding of her body, the anorexic holds sway over an audience both fascinated by the extent of physical change as well as repulsed via their proximity to the body without form.

35. As Kaplan notes, the sexual nature of the disorder's manifestation is implicit in the German term for anorexia: *"Pubertatsmangersucht"*.

36. Hilde Bruch, *The Golden Cage: The Enigma Of Anorexia Nervosa*, Cambridge: Harvard University Press, 1978. Cited Kaplan p.461.

ASIA ARGENTO

THOMAS KRETSCHMANN

LA SINDROME DI STENDHAL

ANNA WITH A DEVIL INSIDE

KLEIN, ARGENTO, & "THE STENDHAL SYNDROME"

Dario Argento's films typically play themselves out as hesitant, impeded detective narratives in which the heroes and heroines are marked by an often terminal inability successfully to discriminate between the truth and falsehood of the evidence they encounter. All that should be good in the world reveals itself as corrupt as icons of normality, authority and care turn out rather to represent perversion, impotence and aggression. Social, cultural and, particularly, familial relationships are prone to inversion as the (biblical) universe of moral order – of distinction, hierarchy and what Janine Chasseguet-Smirgel refers to as the Universal Law[1] – gives way to be replaced for the films' protagonists by the killer's perverse universe in which new and perverse relationships, new and perverse hierarchies and new and perverse meanings and interpretations take hold.

Argento's protagonists have to fight for their understanding in a world which is organised specifically for its denial. When they do come towards a resolution, that resolution typically necessitates an immersion into (literally in the case of Jennifer Corvino in **Phenomena**, 1985), or incorporation of, the killer's perverse world view. The intimacy of the relationship between detective and killer – particularly in those narratives where their functions directly overlap or in which the one becomes the other such as is the case with Anna Manni in **The Stendhal Syndrome** (1996) – implies a complex, shifting connection between individuals and their particular understanding of the world of objects which they inhabit. This scenario in which identities, relationships and positions shift and blend radically lends itself to interpretation through a model which is designed to account for such personal invasions, expulsions and incorporations. Such a model can be found in "object relations theory" of the sort pioneered in England by the psychoanalyst Melanie Klein[2].

Klein pioneered the development of child analysis initially in Austria and significantly in this country. Her clinical and theoretical insights came out of the interpretation of children's play in the context of analysis (the *play technique*). She viewed phantasies expressed in a child's play as communications of the child's unconscious phantasies in a similar way to Freud's focus on the dreams and free associations of adults in analysis. A Kleinian approach offers the critic a challenging alternative to well-established Freudian and Lacanian approaches to film analysis. Indeed, a critical approach drawing on object relations theory immediately departs from "ego-psychology" in that it requires a fundamental shift in analytical focus from the investigation of what happens within the psyche to what happens with the interaction of inner worlds. In other words, as Elizabeth Wright reminds us, a Kleinian approach would privilege the complex and shifting relationship between artist and medium or critic and text.[3]

Kleinian psychoanalysis is founded in part on the assertion that phantasy is in many ways a *precondition* of any engagement with reality. For Kleinians the process of childhood development is organised around the parallel development of the child's understanding of, and relations with, an ongoing series of encounters with objects (people and things). Unlike the work of Anna Freud and her group, Kleinians interpreted the young child's behaviour and relationship to the analyst as involving transferences or reflections of emotional relationships which the child had to his internal images of his parents. These were termed object relationships as such parental relationships were not just based upon the interaction of the child with its external parents, but such experiences of external parents compounded, distorted or enhanced by the child's feelings towards its parents (loves, hates, desires, fears, gratifications and frustrations) and his phantasies about them; about their powers over him and his (or her) powers over the parents (phantasies of omnipotence etc). Successfully passing through certain stages in the development of early object relations (particularly in the first few months after birth) affects the subject's ability to form successful relationships in later life. Objects are investigated, interpreted, incorporated and otherwise interacted with by the child through "unconscious phantasy". Unconscious phantasy is a term developed by Klein and others to account for what R. D. Hinshelwood describes as: "the mental expression of the instinctual impulses and also of defence mechanisms against instinctual impulses."[4] Furthermore, "unconscious phantasies of relationships with objects constitute the mental activity of the newly born infant. These are the primary experiences from which the rest of life, mind and development starts. They are of fundamental importance."[5]

Importantly, Klein departs from Freud here in rejecting the notion that there is a period in which the infant only relates to itself. As Julia Segal puts it: "One of the baby's first actions is to search for the nipple: the baby is born in some sense aware of the need for something outside itself."[6] In other words, "biological activity comes with pre-formed psychological meaning."[7] Klein proposes the existence of a primitive ego which sets up basic defence mechanisms and transforms initial aggressive instincts, and life preserving instincts, through processes which she called "projection" and "introjection".

Mrs Klein developed the account of projection begun by Freud in 1895 and developed by Karl Abraham (notably in 1924), and its meaning has been continually re-examined by Kleinians and others since her death. At its most simple, in projection the subject identifies parts or aspects of itself – usually hated or violent parts – as existing within an external object (commonly another person). Typically this external object is the mother or father or, in a relatively common scenario, a combined (and often horrific) Mother/Father figure. Incidentally, it is the recurrence of such combined figures in early phantasy which prompted Mrs Klein to argue for the presence of pre-genital Oedipal structures – in other words existing earlier than in the Freudian developmental timetable. "Projection," writes Julia Segal, "can be thought of as *perceiving* someone else as having one's own characteristics..." A more active and even violent version of this activity: "projective identification" "involves ... *getting rid of* something belonging to the self into someone else... In other words, in the child's phantasy, hated parts of the self are forced into the mother who is then identified with these parts of the self and hated violently."[8] These phantasies are experienced as real and often physical and the child believes it has actually performed or is in danger of performing the phantasised actions. In this way Kleinian psychoanalysts and psychotherapists acknowledge a deep and important interlocking between a subject's "biological make-up and psychological experience".[9]

Conversely introjection "is a process whereby qualities that belong to an external object are absorbed and unconsciously regarded as belonging to the self. The infant thus creates an ideal object for itself by getting rid of all bad impulses from itself and taking in all it perceives as good from the object."[10] In this way we can see that the child's development is in many ways about the struggle to understand, and thus to position itself, in relation to external objects. This process of object formation – in which every step is earned through a sort of internal struggle – goes through stages. Specifically, objects are not, at first, "clearly delimited and secure in their separateness as they are for the adult."[11] Thus the child goes through a period where it relates to the world through "part objects".

Part objects are what adults would interpret as elements or aspects of a whole person. The mother's breast, for example, typically becomes a part object for the child. In this way it can be argued that the breast takes on a *metonymic* significance, standing in place of the mother herself. The child invests part objects with phantasies which are both positive and negative. In this way, the child shifts between powerful feelings of love and hate for the part object, splitting its identification (as it does its ego) between, the resulting "good" and "bad" objects – in our example a "good breast" and a "bad breast". The good breast is loved for never failing to provide gratification, comfort and satisfaction; the bad breast is the absent good breast perceived as a present bad breast and hated as an imaginary persecutor.

It is important to emphasise that the Kleinian model foregrounds the shifting nature of identification, and thus of object relations. A major difference between Kleinian and Freudian accounts of childhood development is that for many Kleinians the child experiences aspects of the oral, anal and genital phases as overlapping – even as coterminous. For Freud, these phases were entered into one after another in a rather strict sequence; for Klein, the process is much more fluid. Nowhere is this more apparent in Kleinian theory than in the account of the "paranoid-schizoid" and "depressive positions". Even in their naming we are given a suggestion how they interact. Unlike the bounded Freudian phases, Klein saw the child working through different relationships with objects and was aware that an individual could shift back and forth between these relationships throughout its life.

In terms of the child's development, the first of these two situations is the paranoid-schizoid position in which the child's identification is split between good and bad (part) objects. Unable to appreciate that the mother is a full person and, thus, that she embodies contradictions (good and bad), for example, the child lives in fear of the bad breast and idealises the good breast. As Hinshelwood reminds us, the child's earliest experiences are either wholly good with good objects or wholly bad with bad objects. The early ego splits to protect itself from the wholly bad experiences.

The depressive position occurs later in the first year of life when the child begins to be able to integrate its objects. In this way, the child comes to understand that its objects contain both good and bad elements or aspects. Internalised objects are, in this way, now the focus of more ambivalent responses which prompt feelings of guilt in the child over its previous omnipotent, aggressive fantasies towards the good object. These guilty feelings typically cause the child to want to make amends for its previous actions. Once again, it must not be forgotten that an individual may shift between these positions at different times.

As I have already suggested, a Kleinian approach to aesthetics could help to unravel the complexity of the relationship between the artist and his or her medium and that between the critic and his or her object of analysis. In this way, "the prototype for the aesthetic interaction both as regards the artist to his medium and the audience to the art-object is the (unconsciously) felt encounter between infant and mother. The medium of the artist becomes the mother's body... [and] the creative act repeats the experience of separating from the mother." Depending on the type of representation – specifically if it is in some way either fragmented or integrated – this act can take place in the context of either the paranoid-schizoid or the depressive position.[12]

Of course it is also possible to offer a "Kleinian reading" or "Kleinian interpretation" of the content or narrative of an art-object – and such a reading would, of necessity, be coloured by the implications of the relationship of reader and text as outlined above. As a way of attempting both to explicate the theory outlined thus far and to offer a way of using such an approach for the study of horror film narratives I propose the following account of Dario Argento's **The Stendhal Syndrome**.

Argento's film offers a number of approaches which intersect but begin from somewhat different premises. These might include an investigation of the nature of the problem Anna Manni has with art. Thus the so-called "Stendhal Syndrome" of the film's title requires analysis. The narrative of the interaction between Anna and the killer which results in her taking over his murderous rôle and incorporating elements of his personality offers a clear opportunity for a psychoanalytic reading. Likewise, the playing out of Anna's own encounter with psychoanalysis begs attention. A full reading would also need to take into account the perverse implications of the sadomasochistic interactions of the characters, a narrative thread which, in many ways, links all the previous issues. A Kleinian response to all of these issues could involve asking three fundamental questions of the film, its characters, its makers and its spectators. How do we sort out "good" from "bad" or victim from aggressor when we incorporate both and identify at times with either? How can the integration of objects (such as that required for the move from the paranoid-schizoid to the depressive position) be achieved and at what cost to the self in terms of psychological and emotional pain? Here we are using pain in the sense that Kleinians use the term depression. Finally, and most conventionally, is symbol formation and *sublimation* by artistic creativity one of the means by which we do this work of integration?

In *The Apprehension Of Beauty*,[13] Donald Meltzer writes of the relationship between the infant and the good object in terms of the child idealising and being overwhelmed by its beauty. Indeed so unbearably beautiful is the object – the good breast – that it not only dazzles but frightens. A common response to such an overwhelming sensation is to transform it into a situation of primal envy. Feelings of envy are expressed towards the good object just for being good and beautiful and, furthermore, the infant shows that it resents and is angered by its own state of dependence towards it.[14] These feelings often result in oral sadistic attacks on the object. In this way, the symptoms of the "Stendhal Syndrome" enact in one sense at least Anna's inability to contain this central conflict of identification within herself through dreams, through transference with her analyst or through symbolisation – in this case with beautiful paintings in the Uffizi Gallery.

Envy, in the Kleinian sense of the term, obliterates the distinction between good and bad. In this way it implies a fundamental crisis in discrimination (an uncertainty over what is good and what is bad) which is replicated in Anna's confusion over identification. The idea of a crisis in discrimination typically underpins narrative progression in many *gialli* – as Xavier Mendik has persuasively argued from a broadly Lacanian perspective.[15] Indeed the films of Dario Argento are replete with often unsought and frequently perilous encounters with vengeful and aggressive monstrous maternal and paternal figures. The narrative positioning of the three mother/witches in **Inferno** (1980); the homicidal psychic mother in **Trauma** (1994); the paradox – as we shall see – of Anna Manni's absent mother and domineering father in **The Stendhal Syndrome** to name but three instances, all embody a problem of recognising good as good and bad as bad. Similar problems occur in the use of gender confusion across a range of films, and the reversal of other types such as bad priests in films like Fulci's **Don't Torture A Duckling** (1972) and Bido's **Bloodstained Shadow** (1978) serve a not dissimilar purpose. They both confuse the detective in the film's narrative and represent manifestations of aggression from cultural good objects. Indeed it is frequently (although not always) the actions or even merely the simple presence of the detective in the past as a child or in the present as a struggling hero/victim which animates the monstrous into aggressive action. In this way it is even possible to argue that *giallo* narratives use envy unconsciously as a central organising principle.

In **The Stendhal Syndrome**, Anna admits to her psychiatrist an ongoing, complex and terrifying relationship with her internal world. Specifically she is convinced that the killer is inside her, continually growing in power and malevolence, and is threatening to take her over. The idea that introjected good and bad objects are believed actually to be present in (and by) the subject and that these internal objects are performing acts which impact directly and forcefully on the subject's sense of self and of well-being is one of the most important, challenging and controversial interventions of Melanie Klein and her followers. Hinshelwood outlines the curious paradox that lies at its heart:

It seems like a contradiction – an experience which is unconscious... I cannot go into the contradiction of 'unconscious experiencing', except to state how useful it actually is in psychoanalytic theory and practice, and that the emergence of a patient's insight into such experience is both possible and, ultimately, a healing influence... internal objects are deeply involved in processes which may give identity, or create deep rifts within the personal identity of the individual. Identity is thus deeply bound up with the internalization of objects (introjection), with the degree of hostility towards them in the internalization phantasies and the resulting alienation from, or assimilation to, the internalized object. The term 'introjection' denotes a psychic process; but it is linked with – in fact it operates through – an unconscious phantasy in the patient's mind, the subjective experience of taking something in ('internalizing' or, sometimes, 'incorporating' it).[16]

When patients introject and identify with a bad internal object, often their hatred of it means that while they resist and, thus, fail to identify with it properly it remains an alien part of them. With the example of Anna and her introjected bad object (the killer) in mind, I am going to work through an example cited by the psychoanalyst Paula Heimann from her own clinical practice in order to illustrate how patients encounter the problem of identification with a bad internal object.

Heimann's account of "The Woman With A Devil Inside" is particularly instructive for our current purposes in that the patient (a seriously paranoid woman) was an artist and, for her, the result of introjecting a bad object in anger was for that alien object momentarily to take over the creative part of her and to change the way she expressed that creativity. The woman, on her way to her art school, was angered by a poor driver who nearly made her cause an accident. The patient retaliated through a minor act of what would now be called road rage and challenged the other driver, an older "woman who had a red beery face", for her inconsiderate and dangerous behaviour. When the offending driver shrugged the criticism off, the patient insulted her and drove off. During the art class which followed, the patient felt somehow unhappy about the painting she was doing although she couldn't identify exactly what the problem was. It was only when her teacher noted with surprise that her style had completely changed that the woman realised that she had been painting in the style of a "Victorian family album" – quite different from her normal approach. "Something had literally got into her that turned her off from her own apparent intention and diverted her into following a style of someone fifty years ago – that is a much older woman. The explanation offered [by Heimann] is that the older woman in the car who had turned her off the road she had wanted to go along had actually got into her – an introjection, and then a dominance, by the 'bad' object."[17] The patient was so shocked that she went and had three glasses of sherry. Later, she noticed that she had developed three ulcers in her mouth. Paula Heimann's reading connected the drinking – coinciding with angry thoughts about the woman driver – with the development of guilt and the punishing ulcers:

She had carried out her impulse to hurt the woman and was consciously pleased with her success. But unconsciously – as the woman stood for [Heimann] and [the patient's] mother, towards whom she had love impulses as well as hostile ones – she could not bear the injuries she had inflicted on her nor could she remain at a distance from her. She had immediately

*internalized this mother-figure and she had internalized her
in the injured condition for which she felt responsible and
guilty, namely as a worn out, fifty-year-old...*[18]

The bad object, internalized in hatred, dominated the internal
world to the point where the patient became so confused that
she experienced a temporary loss of identity. "Capture by this
internalized object replicated the hostile aggressive
relationship in which the external object had made her
helpless."[19] Throughout **The Stendhal Syndrome**, Anna's
relationship to the killer – initially her external male object –
plays out a similar process. Introjected in hatred, the killer –
now as a bad internal object – increasingly causes Anna to
behave out of character. Having been attacked, Anna
defensively initially projects onto the killer her omnipotent
and aggressive desires for power over the receptive object
although, of course, she also fears them coming back to her
from him. She even tries to play out her phantasies of
omnipotence against her insipid boyfriend and later admits to
desiring to make love like a man.

In Kleinian terms, Anna's response to the fears of
reprisal for her own projected phantasies of omnipotence is to
identify through introjection with the male aggressor who is
both desired and feared. It is important to remember here that
introjection and projection involve a splitting of identification
as an ego defence mechanism. It is safer to become the
aggressor than to be the victim, and Anna's plot trajectory
fluctuates between projective and introjective identifications –
between sadistic and masochistic feelings in herself.
Incidentally, we see similar instances of victims denying their
victimhood by introjecting their aggressors in other films by

Dario Argento – perhaps most memorably in **The Bird With The Crystal Plumage** (1970). Returning to the case of **The Stendhal Syndrome**, however, Anna is unable to reconcile her objects, the introjected male object (the killer) grows as a threat – which is experienced as a *physical sensation* of pain – and eventually comes to dominate her internal life. As we have seen, Kleinians often link psychological operations with direct bodily responses. The dynamic internal world of a patient in which his or her introjected internal objects clash and compete in phantasy is frequently experienced in directly physical terms. Arguably, Anna's attempts at painting emphasise this problem with internal objects. The faces she repeatedly paints have huge black (anal) mouths, almost as if they were openings to evacuate (project) the introjected killer which she cannot accomplish in phantasy. The moment when, after breaking into her flat, he covers those mouths with posters of the paintings from the Uffizi, symbolically blocking off the orifices of her own symbolisations, is also the moment after which her attempts to work through her damaged object relations are futile.

Anna's problem is not limited to her interactions with the killer – even if we can be satisfied with a naturalist reading of the film's narrative and accept what happens as "real" or actual in the film's terms rather than as one long extended phantasy. Given the latter possibility, we can ask of the film whether the killer is actually confronting Anna with the unbearable truth and beauty (the Uffizi paintings) of the good object which her phantasies have distorted and which she finds threatening. Is he actually torturing her or is this her paranoid distortion of how the omnipotent part of herself experiences the truth? Anna obviously has a problematic

relationship with her past, and specifically with her family. We see her with her father, an austere and judgemental patriarch to whose house she retreats only with the greatest reluctance. Of her mother we know and see nothing; and it is around Anna's evident ambivalence towards her familial relationships that the film offers another, more radical avenue of interpretation.

The film could be argued to play out the more general conflict between love and longing for the absent mother as evidenced by Anna's ambivalent attempts to internalize symbolizations of the maternal good object on the one hand, and hatred towards the paternal bad object on the other. This latter is expressed through the introjection of her father – specifically of her father's disapproval – as the punishing

figure of the killer. Her final submission to the internal bad
object signifies in a perverse sense her feelings that "it is now
all daddy, mummy has gone". Her paranoid revenge, killing
male figures coded as sexualised – her new boyfriend – and
authoritative – her psychoanalyst – plays out her inability
either to project or to internalize the destruction of the now
dominant bad object which she further fragments for
apparently easier (although of course ultimately futile)
disposal into discreet aspects of maleness.

Such shifting perspectives, such bewilderments and confusions and mental pains are the stuff of the borderline psychotic's existence and at least fleetingly or in dreams – or indeed in films – may be experienced by any one of us. What Argento's films offer us, then – as do most *gialli* – are moments of identification with just such an experiential realm. Whether we identify with victim or aggressor or whether, as is more accurately the case, our identification shifts along with that of the films' psychotic protagonists, our implication in phantasy offers an – albeit transitory – insight into the working of disturbed minds and more importantly (for here we read the significance of Klein's contribution most strongly) of our still powerful capacity as adults for identification with, and at, an *infantile* level of functioning. In saying this, I am not implying that the films are "infantile", rather that in their complex and ambivalent structures – and in our own complex and ambivalent relationship to those structures – they enact, and expose primary processes of phantasy and early object relations and it is from this that they derive much of their power. Indeed, and in final conclusion, Klein herself recognised (although arguably in a Romantic kind of way) the importance of this relationship between the text and its reader in her own attempts at defining the trajectory of creativity in the arts:

The creative artist makes full use of symbols; and the more they serve to express the conflicts between love and hate, between destructiveness and reparation, between life and death instinct, the more they approach universal form.[20]

NOTES

1. Chasseguet-Smirgel, Janine. *Creativity And Perversion*, London: Free Association Books, 1984.

2. A full exegesis of Kleinian aesthetic theory – let alone of Kleinian and post-Kleinian psychoanalysis as a whole – is clearly beyond the scope of this present paper. Indeed it forms part of an extended research project upon which I am currently engaged. My intention here is simply to present a Kleinian reading of certain features in Argento's films, not to undertake a meta-theoretical mapping of Kleinian thought onto film theory. Such is the function of future publications.

3. Wright, Elizabeth. *Psychoanalytic Criticism: Theory In Practice*, London: Methuen, 1984

4. Hinshelwood, R.D. *A Dictionary Of Kleinian Thought*, London: Free Association Books, 1991, p.32.

5. Hinshelwood, R.D. *Clinical Klein*, London: Free Association Books, 1994, p.28.

6. Segal, Julia. *Melanie Klein*, 1992, p.40–41.

7. Hinshelwood: 1994, p.33.

8. Segal: 1992, p.36–7.

9. Hinshelwood: 1994, p.29.

10. Wright: 1984, p.80.

11. Wright: 1984, p.80.

12. Wright: 1984, p.84.

13. Meltzer, Donald and Harris Williams, Meg. *The Apprehension Of Beauty: The Role Of Aesthetic Conflict In Development, Art And Violence* Perth: Clunie, 1988.

14. The death instinct is deflected by projection into an object which comes to represent the threat of aggression towards the life of the subject.

15. Mendik, Xavier. "Detection And Transgression: The Investigative

Drive Of The Giallo" in *Necronomicon: Book One*, ed. Andy Black, London: Creation, 1996.

16. Hinshelwood: 1994, p.58–9.

17. Hinshelwood: 1994, p.76.

18. Heimann cited in Hinshelwood: 1994, p.76.

19. Hinshelwood: 1994, p.76.

20. Klein, Melanie. "Infantile Anxiety-Situations Reflected In A Work Of Art And In The Creative Impulse", *The Selected Melanie Klein*, ed. Juliet Mitchell, London: Penguin, 1986, p.299.

LIST OF ILLUSTRATIONS